PRACTICAL CATALOGUING WITH AACR-II

PRACTICAL CATALOGUING WITH AACR-II

Compiled & Edited by
Prof. Mohd. Sabir Husain
Former Chairman
Department of Library & Information Science
Aligarh Muslim University, Aligarh
and
Dr. Jamal Ahmad Siddiqui
Dy. Librarian, University Library & Head
Department of Library & Information Science
Ch. Charan Singh University, Meerut

Ess Ess Publications
New Delhi

PRACTICAL CATALOGUING WITH AACR-II

ISBN : 978-93-87698-03-1

First Published 2018

Published by:
Ess Ess Publications
4831/24, Ansari Road,
Darya Ganj,
New Delhi-110 002.
INDIA
Phones: 23260807, 41563444
Fax: 41563334
E-mail: info@essessreference.com
www.essessreference.com

Cover Design by *Patch Creative Unit*

Printed and bound in India

Dedicated to

PARENTS

Contents

Contents

Preface

The libraries have undergone remarkable changes in the present era of Information Technology and digitization advancement due to impact on use of computer in libraries. With the passage of time, computer is being employed in almost all library operations, like OPAC, Computerized catalogue, etc. Whether the catalogue is computerized or is in the form of card, the cataloguing rules as provided in Anglo-American Cataloguing Rules - II (AACR - II) published in 1978 are being followed extensively in libraries in India. These rules are equally workable in cataloguing of English language as well as in Hindi and Urdu language books. A number of illustrated guide books for English language books as well as Hindi language books are available but with illustrations of English books. In Urdu, however, a book entitled **'Katalog Sazi Ki Teknik Ka Ek Jaiza'** was published by Haji Mohd. Zubair, Former Asstt. Librarian, Maulana Azad Library, Aligarh Muslim University in 1963 with illustrations of Urdu books. It was based on 'ALA Rules for Author and Title Entries' published in 1949 by ALA, Chicago as it was the only cataloguing code being followed in those days.

Sometime in 1987-88, Mrs. Kalpna Dasgupta, the then National Librarian, National Library of India, Kolkata narrated her hard experience in cataloguing of Urdu books even though the Urdu qualified persons were recruited in the Library but problems and difficulties were being faced. The matter was given serious thought. It was discussed with the teachers in the Department of Library & Information Science, A.M.U., Aligarh. It was thought to introduce Urdu as well as Hindi books cataloguing as part of B.Lib.& Inf. Sc. Cataloguing Practical paper. The opinion of Prof. P.B. Mangla, internationally renowned Library Scientist and expert member of Board of Studies of the Department was sought who appreciated the proposal and agreed to recommend the introduction of Hindi and Urdu books cataloguing as part of Cataloguing Practical paper. Its teaching was started at B.Lib. & I.Sc. level in 1988-89 and is still continuing.

It was thought appropriate to bring out illustrated books separately in English, Hindi and Urdu language which will serve as guide to students and College & University libraries.

We are thankful to our friends and well-wishers for their help, suggestions and encouragement.

Thanks are also due to Mr. S. Riaz Abbas and Mr. Nasruddin for extending great assistance in bringing out the book.

If the readers find any error and omission, they are requested to bear with us 'To err is human'. Their comments and suggestions for improving the book in the future edition are welcome.

Last but not least, we are thankful to the Publisher for nicely publishing the book on time in proper attractive format.

Mohd. Sabir Husain
Jamal Ahmad Siddiqui

1

The Skeleton of the Card Catalogue

The size of catalogue card is 5 inch in width and 3 inch in height Or 12½ cm. width and 7½ cm. in height. The Ist vertical line is called 'First indention' and 2nd vertical drawn in parallel to Ist vertical leaving 0.5 inch space is called 'Second indention'. The Ist horizontal line at the 'Top' leaving 3-line space is called 'Heading line' or 'Author line'. At the bottom of the card, one 'hole' is provided in the centre on the last visible line, meant for filing of the card in the catalogue tray of catalogue cabinet.

The following items, placed in 3 classes, are to be picked up from the book through collation for cataloging:

I. DESCRIPTIVE INFORMATION

- Author's name
- Title / sub-title / alternate title, if any
- Author's statement and Edition
- Imprint:
  - — Place of publication
  - — Publisher's name
  - — Year of publication

II. PHYSICAL OR COLLATION INFORMATION

- Number of pages or number of volumes
- Size of the book
- Series statement, if any
- Notes statement, if any

III. LOCATION INFORMATION

- Class No.
- Book No.
- Accession No.

SKELETON CARD

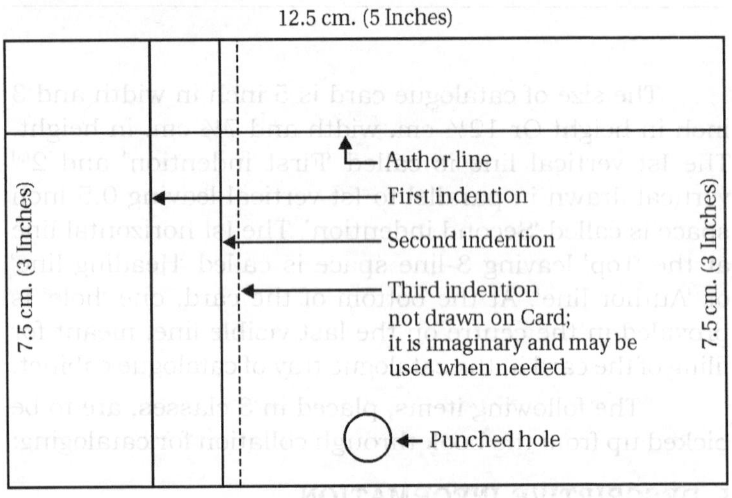

Class No. Book No.	Author's name	
Accession No.	....	Title : sub-title (if any) ..../ author's statement.............. -. Edition. – Place : Publisher.............., Year Pages / Vol. : ill. (if any) ; size – (Series) if any. Notes, if any. .... Tracing ....

ILLUSTRATION OF MAIN ENTRY

394 K 7	Ansari, Abdul Basir	card 3
132189		History of India: Mughal period / Abdul Basir Ansari. – 2nd ed. – New Delhi : Oriental Book House, 1987 v, 190 p. : ill. ; 20 cm. – (Indo-Pakistan series; 12). 1. India – History. 2. Title. 3. Series.

2

Continued Card / Extension Card

When the space on the Main Entry (ME) Card is exhausted to contain more relevant information of the book being catalogued, the next Card is to be used as 'continued card' for providing the remaining information. On the last line at the bottom of the card from the hole in the centre, Continued on next card is mentioned.

On the next Card (i.e. on the continued card), write the Class No. and Book No. as usual. Heading of the ME is to be started from the 1st indention on the Author's line. Then year of publication of the book is given. Write within parenthesis card number as (Card 2). Thereafter, leave 3 lines and furnish the remaining information on the 4th line as shown in the illustration.

ILLUSTRATION

C9D8'p44'N83
M 4
National High Energy Physics Seminar (*3rd : Pune : 1983*)

High temperature phenomena and production : proceedings of the third National High Energy Physics seminar held at Pune July 16 – 18, 1983 / edited by Mukesh K. Srivastava and Vijay K. Malhotra – Pune :

(Continued on next card)

Continued card

C9D8 'p44'N83
M 4
National High Energy Physics Seminar (3rd : Pune : 1983).

High temperature phenomena and production. 1984. (Card 2)
Indian Institute of Thermodynamics, 1984.

vi, 395 p. : ill. ; 26 x 11 cm. – (Thermodynamics seminar & symposia series ; 6).

1. Thermodynamics 2. Srivastava, Mukesh K., ed. 3. Malhotra, Vijay K., jt.ed.

3
Reference Entry

Reference entry is the one which asks the users of the catalogue to go to the heading referred to find the requisite information or book. Such entries are provided in a catalogue to facilitate the users to have an access to the required heading under which the book is available. According to AACR – II, whenever the name of a person or corporate body or the title of a work is or may reasonably be, known under a form that is not used as heading or uniform title, refer from that form to the one under which the related one is entered. This is accomplished by providing 'Reference entry'. Reference entries are of the following kinds:

- 'See' reference entries
- 'See also' reference entries
- 'Explanatory' reference entries

SEE REFERENCE ENTRIES

See reference entry is the one that directs the users from the heading under which no requisite material exists to the heading under which the information or title is available.

Illustrations

From real name to pseudonym

Srivastava, Dhanpat Rai

see Prem Chand

Subject reference entry

Sea mosses

see Algae

Seaweeds

see Algae

U.N.E.S.C.O.

see Unesco

USA

see United States

NATO

see North Atlantic Treaty Organization

See also Reference Entry

This is an entry which directs the users to refer from the heading under which the requisite material is available to the other heading containing the related material or information.

Algae

see also Marine Plants

Marine plants

see also Algae

British Iron and Steel Research Association

see also Iron and Steel Institute

Iron and Steel Institute

see also British Iron and Steel Research Association

Explanatory Reference Entry

As per rule No.26.4C of AACR – II, whenever more detail than a simple 'see' or 'see also' reference is required, a description or explanation is given in an entry. This is known as Explanatory Reference entry.

Illustrations

	Arabian nights	
	For separately published parts of this collection, see Ali Baba Sindbad the sailor etc. etc.	

For Joint / Shared pseudonym

	Dannay, Frederick	
	For works of this author written in collaboration with Manfred Lee, see Queen, Ellery	

	Lee, Manfred	
	For works of this author written in collaboration with Frederick Dannay, see Queen, Ellery	

For author using several pseudonyms and real name

	Paine, Lauren	
	For works of this author written under pseudonyms, see Andrews, A.A. Benton, Will Bosworth, Frank Bradford, Will Bradley, Concho	

	Benton, Will
	For works of this author written under his real name, see Paine, Lauran For works written under his other pseudonyms, see Andrews, A.A. Bosworth, Frank Bradford, Will Bradley, Concho

	Bosworth, Frank
	For works of this author written under his real name, see Paine, Lauran For works written under his other pseudonyms, see Andrews, A.A. Benton, Will Bradford, Will Bradley, Concho

Bradford, Will

For works of this author written under his real name, see

Paine, Lauran

For works written under his other pseudonyms, see

Andrews, A.A.

Benton, Will

Bosworth, Frank

Bradley, Concho

Bradford, Concho

For works of this author written under his real name, see

Paine, Lauran

For works written under his other pseudonyms, see

Andrews, A.A.

Benton, Will

Bosworth, Frank

Bradford, Will

4

Personal Author

Personal authors, as defined by AACR – II, are the persons chiefly responsible for the creation of the intellectual or artistic contents of a work. They can be placed in 2 classes, namely :

- One Personal Author
- More than one Personal Author

ONE PERSONAL AUTHOR

As per AACR – II, rule No.21.4A Main entry (ME) is to be made under the author and according to rule No. 22.1. choose, as the basis of the heading for a person; the name by which he/she is commonly identified or known; may be person's real name, pseudonym, title of nobility, nickname etc.

- William Shakespeare is to be entered in the heading of main entry as Shakespeare, William
- Tariq Ahmad Ansari to be entered as Ansari, Tariq Ahmad
- Arjun S. Dasgupta to be entered as Dasgupta, Arjun S.
- Raja Ram to be entered as Raja Ram
- Mansoor Ali to be entered as Mansoor Ali
- Ram Babu to be entered as Ram Babu

- Ram Babu Saxena to be entered as Saxena, Ram Babu

PERSONAL AUTHOR AND EDITOR & COMPILER, ETC.

When the names of author, editor or compiler are printed on the 'Title-Page' of the book, the author is to be chosen for the heading of the Main entry. The name of the editor or compiler is to be given in the area of responsibility of catalogue entry after the author's name. Added entry is to be provided under the heading of the editor or compiler.

Illustrations of catalogue entries are given in the forthcoming pages in the book.

5

More Than One Author

The works of collaboration by two or more authors are known as the works of 'Joint authorship' or 'Shared authorship'. According to AACR – II, the collaboration between two or more persons or bodies performing the same kind of activity of the creation of the contents of an item are known as 'Shared authorship'. Such works can be placed in two categories:

(A) Principal responsibility indicated

(B) Principal responsibility NOT indicated

A. PRINCIPAL RESPONSIBILITY INDICATED

Showing of principal responsibility can be placed in 2 categories:

(a) Indication on the Title-Page by using words or phrases like; 'with collaboration of _________' or 'with the assistance of _______' ; as for example, "Manohar Lal Joshi with collaboration of Kuldeep Singh Rathore" — Joshi is Principal author

(b) Indication by Print or Type on Title-Page; as for example, "Manohar Lal Joshi and KULDEEP SINGH RATHORE — Rathore is Principal author.

According to AACR – II, rule No.21.6B1, main entry is to be made under Rathore, Kuleep Singh and in the author responsibility area, after title as "Manohar Lal

Joshi and Kuldeep Singh Rathore" to be mentioned.

But when the number of authors exceeds three, main entry is to be made under Principal author (Rathore, Kuldeep Singh) and in the area of author responsibility, the name the first-named author (Manohar Lal Joshi) after title statement, 3 dots ... are given along-with [et al.] in square bracket. Added entry is to be made under the first-named author.

B. PRINCIPAL RESPONSIBILITY NOT INDICATED

When two or three authors collaborate and NONE is indicated as Principal author, main entry is to be made under the first-named author as per rule No.216C1 with added entries under the other authors.

FOUR OR MORE AUTHORS

In the work by four or more authors with NONE indicated as Principal author, main entry as per rule No.21.6C2 is to be made under title of the book on the author-line from the 1st indention with continuation on the 2nd line leaving 2 blank spaces till the last item. Leaving 2 blank spaces from 2nd indention is imaginary third indention and is known as 'Hanging Indention'. In the main entry after 'Title of the book', 3 dots ... are mentioned and thereafter within square bracket [et al.] is written. Added entry is made under the first-named author with no added entry under other authors.

Illustrations of such catalogue entries are given in the forth-coming pages of the book.

6

Editorial Direction

Dictionaries, Encyclopedias, Books containing writings, essays, collection, extracts, etc. "With Collective Title" and "Without Collective Title" are catalogued as per set of rules given under rule No.21.7 of AACR – II.

Such books with Collective Titles edited or compiled by person or group of persons, Dictionaries, Encyclopedias, etc. according to rule No.21.7B are entered under title in 'Hanging indention' in which case title is written on author line and is continued after leaving 2 spaces on subsequent lines from 2nd indention till the last item of imprint. Pages, illustrations, size, etc. are mentioned on next line from 2nd indention. Added entries for Editor or compiler are made as usual.

Books Without Collective Title, as per rule No.21.7C are entered on the basis of information of first mentioned title on the Title-Page of the book.

7

Sacred scriptures

Sacred Scriptures refer to those religious books of different religions which are not attributable to persons or religious groups as their authors. These, for example, include Bible, Shrimad Gita, Vedas, Koran, Gurugranth Saheb, Upanishads, Jaina Agama granth, Avesta, Talmud, Tripataka, etc.

AACR – II, prescribes cataloguing rule No. 21.37, 25.17–25.18 to make main entry under title and Uniform titles for scriptures. Respective rules for the following may be followed given in AACR – II for constructing the main specific heading.

The examples of such headings are given below:

Heading	**Rule No.**
Bible	25.18A
Talmud	25.18B
Tripataka	25.18F
Vedas	25.18G
Upanishads	25.18H
Jaina Agama	25.18J
Avesta	25.18K
Koran	25.18M

Some illustrations of cataloguing of Sacred Scriptures are given in the pages that follow.

8

Pseudonym

Pseudonym is a name assumed by an author to conceal or obscure his or her real identity for one reason or the other. Problems of pseudonym can be placed into 3 classes:

I. One Pseudonym

II. Shared or Joint Pseudonyms

III. Several Pseudonyms

I. One Pseudonym : This refers to such pseudonymous authors who consistantly write books under one pseudonym. Examples are:

—	George Orwell	: Pseudonym
	Eric Arthur Blair	: Real name
—	Prem Chand	: Pseudonym
	Dhanpat Rai Srivastava	: Real name

As per AACR – II rule No. 22.2C1, if all the works of a person appear under one pseudonym and he or she is predominantly identified by it, choose the pseudonym for heading of Main entry. Reference entry from the Real name to the pseudonym is to be made.

II. Shared or Joint Pseudonym : This refers to such Pseudonymous authorship where Two or more authors adopt *ONE* pseudonym jointly, such as for examples: Frederic Dannay and Manfred Lee who jointly adopted Ellery Queen as a Joint Pseudonym.

In accordance with rule No. 21.6D, Main entry is to be made under the Joint or Shared pseudonym and Explanatory Reference entries are to be made under the heading of both the authors.

III. Several Pseudonyms : This is concerned with author who writes books by adopting several pseudonyms and also writes books under the Real name.

Example:

The Real author John Creasey used several pseudonyms in different books as given below:

Gordon Ashe

Michael Halliday

J.J. Marric

Anthony Morton,

Jeremy York and the author also used his Real name.

As per rule of AACR-II, when an author who has used several pseudonyms and is not prominently known by any of his adopted pseudonyms, the heading of the Main entry will be the pseudonym printed on the book being catalogued and reference entries are to be made from Real name and other pseudonyms to each other. But when an author adopting several pseudonyms is prominently known by a particular pseudonym, that pseudonym is to be chosen for the heading of the Main entry and Explanatory Reference entries are to be constructed in accordance with rule No. 26.D1.

Illustrations of all these 3 classes of Pseudonyms have been given on the forthcoming pages of the book.

9

Anonymous Works

These are the works of 'unknown authorship'. AACR – II mentions in rule No.25.4C that if the original language of an anonymous work created before 1501 is not written in Greek language nor in Roman script, use an established title of English and enter under the Uniform title at the heading of the Main entry. The Glossary as given in Appendix 'D' defines the particular title by which such a work is to be identified. It further describes the Conventional Collective Title used to collocate publications of an author, composer or corporate body containing several works or extracts etc. from several works...

It laid down to use the following Uniform title for the folowing:

- Arabian Nights
- Book of Dead, etc.

Arabian nights, amongst all the anonymous works is most popular anonymous classics which is the collection of stories like Ali Baba, Sindbad the Sailor, etc. as mentioned under rule No.25.6B for several parts. Reference entry for 'Sindbad the Sailor' which is one of the stories of Arabian nights, is given as example:

EXPLANATORY REFERENCE ENTRIES

	Arabian night	
	For separately published stories from this collection, see Ali Baba Sindbad the Sailor etc.	

Arabian nights is a collection of stories which is to be entered under uniform title 'Arabian nights'. An illustration is given below:

ONE THOUSAND AND ONE NIGHT

Edited by
Richard Samuel

Adel Reidel Publishing Co.
London

1901

- Pages : i-v and 1-390
- Size : 21.25 centimeters

Arabian nights

One thousand and one nights / edited by Richard Samuel. – London : Adel Reidel Publishing, 1901.

v. 399 p. ; 22 cm.

1. Short stories collection. 2. Samuel, Richard, ed. 3. Title

10

Collection

This covers such works which contain contribution by different writers under a 'Collective Title' or 'Without Collective Title', indicating the contribution of each writer.

As per glossary of AACR – II, the Collection is the work, if by one author : three or more independent works or parts of works published together and if by more than one author, two or more independent works but **NOT** written for the same occasion for publication in hand. AACR – II, places such works in two categories, namely (i) Works published 'With Collective Title' and (ii) Works published 'Without Collective Title'. Dr. S.R. Ranganathan has called works of category (i) as 'Ordinary Composite' works and those of category (ii) as 'Artificial Composite' works.

Illustration of category (i) With Collection Title is given below:

FINE ARTS TO-DAY

Edited by

Dr. Charles Bundock

Wadley & Ginns & Co.
LONDON

1972

Other information:

- Class No. N
- Book No. L2
- Pages : i-v and 1-236
- Part – I : Sculpture by James Walter
  Class No. ND
- Part – II : Graphic Arts by Frazer King
  Class No. NM
- Part – III : Painting by James Newton
  Class No. NQ

Main Entry

N L 2	Fine arts / edited by Charles Bundock. London –
125312	Wadley & Ginns, 1972. v., 236 p. : ill. ; 22 cm. Contents : pt. 1. Sculpture / by James Walter – pt.2. Graphic arts / by Frazer King – pt. 3. Painting / by James Newton. 1. Arts 2. Bundock, Charles, ed. 3. Title

Added entries (AE) for the book will be made as usual. And for each author (contributor), 'In' analytical entries as prescribed according to rule No.13.5B of AACR-II, will be provided, as illustrated below:

Title Analytical Entry

N L 2	Sculpture / by James Walter. – pt.1 : ill. ; 22 cm.
	In : Fine arts / edited by Charles Bundock – London : Wadley & Ginns, 1972.

Author Analytical Entry

N L 2	Walter, James
	Sculpture / by James Walter – pt. 1 : ill. ; 22 cm. *In* : Fine arts / edited by Charles Bundock – London : Wadley & Ginns, 1972.

Category (ii) : Without Collective Title

'Published together' and 'Bound together' works are included under this category. AACR – II, rule No.21.7C prescribes to enter under the heading appropriate to the first named work given in the chief source of information.

Illustration :

CURRICULUM OF UNIVERSITY EDUCATION

by

Dr. Sohan Lal Gupta

AUDIO VISUALS IN ADULT EDUCATION

by

Dr. Murari Lal Awasthi

EDUCATION FOR RURAL COMMUNITY

by

Dr. Roshan Lal Jha

BHARAT PRAKASHAN BHANDAR

ROHTAK

1985

Other information :

- Class No. No. T4:2
- Book No. M 5
- Pages : i-v, 6-139, 142-325 and 328-410
- Size : 22 centimeters
- Accession No. 122123
- These works have been published together with the consent of Copy-right holders

Main Entry

T4:2 M 5	Gupta, Sohan Lal
133215	Curriculum of University education / by Sohan Lal Gupta, Audio visuals in adult education / by Murari Lal Awasthi, Education for rural community / by Roshan Lal Jha. – Rohtak : Bharart Prakashan Bhandar, 1985. 139, 142-325, 328-410 p. ; 22 cm. 1. University education 2. Title 3. Awasthi, Murari Lal, Audio... 4. Jha, Roshan Lal, Education...

Added Entries for University education and Title, as usual, are to be made.

AE (Name-Title) for 2nd work

T4:2 M 5	Awasthi, Murari Lal Audio visuals in adult education Gupta, Sohan Lal
	Curriculum of university education / by Sohan Lal Gupta, Audio visuals in adult education / by Murari Lal Awasthi, Education for rural community / by Roshan Lal Jha. – Rohtak : Bharat Prakashan Bhandar, 1985. pp. 142-325; 22 cm.

AE (Name-Title) for 3rd work

T4:2 M 5		Jha, Roshan Lal. Education for rural community Gupta, Sohan Lal
		Curriculum of university education / by Sohan Lal Gupta, Audio visuals in adult education / by Murari Lal Awasthi, Education for rural community / by Roshan Lal Jha. – Rohtak : Bharat Prakashan Bhandar, 1985. pp. 328-410; 22 cm.

BOUND TOGETHER BOOKS

Sometime 2 or more independent books are bound together in one volume in a library. AACR-II, vide its rule No.21.7C prescribes to make ME on the basis of 1st bound book, giving the information of the remaining bound book/books. In the ME of the remaining books to be constructed, the Class No. and Book No. of the 1st book are to be given.

Illustration:

INTRODUCTION TO
IRRIGATIONAND DRAINAGE WORK

by
Dr. Islam Ahmad Rehmani
(*Second Edition*)

EHSAN BOOK STORE
Meerut

1973

SUB-SOIL WATER AND EARTHWORK EXCAVATION

by
Dr. Jai Prasad Bindal

Manohar Pustak Bhandar
Sonipat

1968

Other Information :

***First Work* :**

- Class No. D2
- Book No. L 3
- Pages : i-iv and 1-152
- Size : 22 centimeters
- Accession No. 122114
- Thouroughly illustrated.

***Second Work* :**

- Class No. D284:7
- Book No. K 8
- Pages : i-v and 6-152
- Size : 22 centimeters
- Accession No. 143211
- Illustrated.

Note: First and second works have been bound together in the library

Main entry

D2 K 3	Rehmani, Islam Ahmad
122114	Introduction to irrigation and drainage work / by Islam Ahmad Rehmani. – 2nd ed. – Meerut : Ehsan Book Store, 1973. vi, 152 p. : ill. ; 22 cm. With : Sub-soil water and earthwork excavation / by Jai Prasad Bindal. – Sonipat : Manohar Pustak Bhandar, 1968. 1. Irrigation 2. Title

ME for the 2nd Bound work:

D2 K 3	Bindal, Jai Prasad,
143211	Sub-soil water and earthwork excavation / by Jai Prasad Bindal. – Sonipat : Manohar Pustak Bhandar, 1968. 152 p. : ill. ; 22 cm. With : Introduction to irrigation and drainage work / by Islam Ahmad Rehmani. – 2nd ed. – Meerut : Ehsan Book Store, 1973. 1. Earthwork excavation 2. Title

Added entries for the 1st work and 2nd work, as usual, will be constructed.

11

Corporate Bodies

Books, reports, etc., written by persons employed or holding charge of official positions in Corporate bodies like associations, societies, institutions, firms, government & its agencies and constituents, seminars, meetings, conference, etc. are entered under the concerned organisations or group of persons identified by a particular name of persons according to AACR - II as per rules provided in Chapter 24.

Corporate bodies can broadly be placed in the following categories:

- Government & its agencies
- Meetings, Conferences, Congress, Symposia, etc.
- Institutions, Associations, Societies, Universities, Religious bodies
- Rules for Radio Stations, TV centers, Exhibitions, Fairs etc. are also provided.

Government

- Central Govt. : Govt. of India
- State Govt. : Govt. of Uttar Pradesh
- Local Govt. : Nagar Nigam
  Municipal Board
  District Board

Panchayati Raj, etc.

Conference, Seminar, Symposium, etc.

- Technical Information Centers Administrative Conference
- Biology of Whale International Conference
- International Geography Seminar (held in 1956 at Aligarh Muslim University).

Institutions, Associations, Museums, Universities, Religious bodies, etc.

- Indian Science Congress
- Aligarh Muslim University
- Khuda Bakhsh Oriental Public Library, Patna
- Indian Library Association
- Delhi Door Darshan
- British Museum
- Library of Congress
- Vatican Council, etc.

The heading to be used in the Main entry of some selected Corporate Bodies are given below:

- India. *Ministry of Finance.*

  India. *Union Public Service Commission.*
- India. *Advisory Committee for Libraries.*
- India. *University Grants Commission.*
- India. *High Commission (Canada)*
- India. *High Commission (Sri Lanka)*
- India. *Constitution.*
- India. *Lok Sabha.*
- India. *Rajya Sabha.*
- India. *Supreme Court.*
- India. *Planning Commission.*
- United Nations Organisation.

- World University Service.
- North Atlantic Treaty Organisation. (NATO)
- Unesco.
- Uttar Pradesh. *Vidhan Sabha.*
- Uttar Pradesh. *Vidhan Parishad.*
- Uttar Pradesh. *High Court.*
- Aligarh. *Nagar Nigam.*
- Aligarh. *District Panchayat.*
- Aligarh. *Civil Court*

Head of State

AACR – II provided rules vide 24.20B for constructing the heading for Emperor, King, President of Republic prescribing the – Name of the country, Name of the Office, Duration of tenure and Name of the Head of the State as illustrated below:

- India. *Mughal Emperor (1556-1605) : Mohd. Jalaluddin Akbar*
- Gt. Brit. *King (1910-1936) : George V*
- India. *President (1550-1962 : Rajendra Prasad)*
- Pakistan. *President (1960-1966 : Ayyub Khan)*
- Gt. Brit. *Queen (1952 - : Elizabeth II)*
- Uttar Pradesh. *Governor (2015 - :)*

Head of Government

AACR – II Provided rules vide rule No.24.20C, prescribing to use the name of the country or Pradesh, Office in the heading as illustrated below:

- India. *Prime Minister.*
- United Nations. *Secretary General.*
- Madhya Pradesh. *Chief Minister.*
- Aligarh. *Mayor.*

CONFERENCES, CONGRESSES, SYMPOSIA, MEETINGS, ETC.

These are the groups of experts, subject specialists assembled at a common platform for deliberations, on a theme or subject so as to formulate and express opinion or sentiments. These may be periodic or adhoc (non-periodic) with or without specific name. Some examples are given below:

1. International Religion Conference, held on 1963 at Varanasi.
2. International Geography Seminar, held in July, 1956 at Aligarh Muslim University.
3. Fifth All India Congress of Cytology and Genetics, held at Bhubneswar in October, 1981.
4. Senior Citizens Meet held at Bombay in 1988 (examples of without specific names).

AACR – II laid down rule No.24.7 for the heading of main entry. The heading is to consist of the name of Seminar / Conference / Symposium etc., followed by starter bracket then Number of the Conference, if any, : Year of holding : Place as illustrated below for the above 4 titles:

1. International Religion Conference (*1963 : Varanasi*)
2. International Geography Seminar (*1956 : Aligarh Muslim University*)
3. All India Congress of Cytology and Genetics (*5th : 1984 : Bhubneswer*)
4. Senior Citizens Meet (*1988 : Bombay*)

An illustration of ME is given for easy understanding:

2:51fp1,N75 L 5	International Study Conference on Classification	
132541	Research (3rd : 1975 : Bombay). Ordering system for global information network : proceedings / edited by A. Neelameghan. – Bangalore : FID / CR and Sarda Ranganathan Endowment for Library Science, 1975. vii, 315 p. ; 25 cm. – (FID Publication; 553). 1. Library Classification-Research 2. Neelameghan, A., ed. 3. Title 4. Series. ○	

INSTITUTION

Another category of Corporate authorship is 'Institution' which covers Universities, Colleges, Museums, Libraries, Councils, Boards, Societies, Associations, Radio and Television Stations, Business Organisations, Courts, Exhibitions, Fairs, Churches, etc. Names of some institutions are given below:

- National Library, Kolkata
- Indian Science Congress
- Aligarh Muslim University
- University Grants Commission (India)
- Indian Library Association
- Nehru Museum, Delhi
- Rajasthan Public Service Commission
- National Council of Educational Research and Training (NCERT)
- Supreme Court (India)
- Indian Institute of Public Administration
- League of Nations, Geneva
- Unesco, Paris

- International Federation of Library Associations and Institutions (IFLA)
- Delhi Doordarshan etc.

As per AACR – II, rules Nos. 24.13 and 24.14, ME is to be made under the direct name of the body; if needed, it may be individualized by giving the location / place. Illustrations of ME are given below:

***Illustration* of ME : No.1**

T2:8 'N71 L 1	National Council of Educational Research and Training (India)
122321	Review of educational administration in secondary schools : 1950 – 71 / edited by Mahendra Singh Grover. – New Delhi : Manager of Publications NCERT, 1971. viii, 213 p. : ill. ; 22 cm. 1. Education review 2. Education-administration 3. Title

Illustration No.2

X5:8 H 3	League of Nations. Economic Financial and Transit Department. Geneva.
124531	Trade relations between free market and controlled economics / League of Nations, economic financial and transit Department. – Geneva : League of Nations, 1943 viii, 213 p. : ill. ; 22 cm. 1. Free-market trade 2. Controlled economics 3. Title

12
Serials

Any publication that is published in successive parts intended to be continued indefinitely and these parts together form a volume with its number and issue number, is a serial. As per AACR – II, serial is a publication in any medium issued in successive parts bearing numerical or chronological designations and are intended to be continued indefinitely. Serials include periodicals, newspapers, annuals (reports, yearbooks, etc.); journals, memoirs, proceedings, transactions, numerical series etc.

Cataloguing rules have been given in Chapter 12 of AACR – II. Normally, the main entry of serial is made under the title together with information relating to volume number, year of publication, place, Sponsoring body/ Publishers, if given, first volume published with year and number, volume number with year of the subscription by the Library; also information if a particular issue or volume is not available in the Library, volume that is not published in a particular year. The number of the current volume is mentioned with black lead pencil.

Some difficulties and problems also happen to occur in the publication of serials. They are enumerated below:

- Continuation, continued by

- Merger, merged with
- Amalgamation, amalgamated by
- Split
- Absorption, absorbed by
- Reproduction
- Edition
- Translation
- Suspension
- Supplements
- Index, etc.

For any of the above problem, rule No.12.7B7 of AACR – II may be consulted where illustrations have been given.

Examples of Serial involving Continuation and Absorption is given below as an illustration.

Title Page

QUARTERLY JOURNAL OF SCIENCE Vol. I 1976   **BRITISH SOCIETY OF SCIENCE** LONDON

- Class No. Am56,76
- It was started in 1976 with one volume to be completed in one non-calendar year.
- No volume was published in 1978-79
- In 1980 the title was changed to "Scientific Monthly" with no change in volume numbering.
- After publication of Vol. 6, this periodical was absorbed by periodical "Science" Class No. Am56,N63
- Library has complete set of first journal

Main Entry-I

Am56,76	Quarterly journal of science/ British Society of	
		Science. – Vol. I (1976/77) – V.4 (1979/80). – London : British Society of Science, 1976-1980.
		4 v.
		No. Vol. published during 1978/79.
		Continued by : Scientific monthly.
		1. Science—periodicals. 2. British Society of
	Science.	
		O

Main Entry-II (On Continuation and Absorption)

Am56,8	Scientific monthly / British Society of Science – Vol.	
		5 (1980/81). – London : British Society of Science, 1980 –
		2 v.
		Continues : Quarterly journal of Science.
		Absorbed by : Science.
		1. Science—periodicals. 2. British Society of
	Science.	

Main Entry-III (On Absorbed) in 'Science'

Am56,63	Science / British Society of Science – Vol. 20 (1982).	
		– London : British Society of Science, 1963 –
		Quarterly.
		Absorbed : Scientific monthly, 1981/82

CATALOGUING EXERCISES AND PROBLEMS

Personal author Problem No. 01

Single

RELIGIOUS THOUGHT
AND
LIFE IN INDIA

Vedism, Brahmanism and Hinduism

by

Mornier William

ORIENTAL BOOKS REPRINTS CORPORATION

New Delhi

1974

- Class No. 294
- Book No. L 4
- Pages : i-v and 6-520
- size : 22¼ centimeters
- Accession No. 138878

294 L 4	William, Mornier
138878	Religious thought and life in India : Vedism, Brahmanism and Hinduism / by Mornier William. – New Delhi : Oriental Book Reprints, 1974. 520 p. ; 23 cm. 1. Religions – India. 2 Title

294 L 4	RELIGIONS – INDIA
	William, Mornier Religious thought and life in India : Vedism, Brahmanism and Hinduism / by Mornier William. – New Delhi : Oriental Book Reprints, 1974. 520 p. ; 23 cm.

294 L 4	Religious thought and life in India William, Mornier
	Religious thought and life in India : Vedism, Brahmanism and Hinduism / by Mornier William. – New Delhi : Oriental Book Reprints, 1974. 520 p. ; 23 cm.

Personal author Problem No. 02

Multi-volume Book

THE HISTORY OF FREEDOM MOVEMENT IN INDIA

by

Dr. TARA CHAND

Foreward by

Prof. Humayun Kabir

Publication Division

Govt. of India

Delhi

1961

- Class No. V44:51B47
- Book No. K1.1 – K1.3
- Accession Nos. 18913 & 18914
- The work is in 3 volumes
- Vol. I – Freedom Struggle
- Vol. II – Freedom Fighters
- Vol. III – Freedom Movement
- Liberation Movement Series No. XV
- Vol. II is not available in the library

V44:51 B47 K1.1-K 1.3	Tara	Chand
18913-14		The history of freedom movement in India / by Tara Chand; foreword by Humayun Kabir. – Delhi : Publication Division, Govt. of India, 1961-1972. 3 v. ; 22 cm. – (Liberation movement series ; 15) Contents : v.1. Freedom Struggles – v.2 Freedom fighters – v.3. Freedom movement. Library lacks vol.2 (1967) 1. Freedom movement 2. Title 3. Series

V44:51B47 K1.1-K 1.3	Tara	FREEDOM MOVEMENT Chand
		The history of freedom movement in India / by Tara Chand; foreword by Humayun Kabir. – Delhi : Publication Division, Govt. of India, 1961-1972. 3 v. ; 22 cm. – (Liberation movement series ; 15) Contents : v.1. Freedom Struggle – v.2 Freedom fighters – v.3. Freedom movement. Library lacks vol.2 (1967)

V44:51 'B47 The History of freedom movement
K1.1-K 1.3 Tara Chand

The history of freedom movement in India / by Tara Chand; foreword by Humayun Kabir. – Delhi : Publication Division, Govt. of India, 1961-1972.

3 v. ; 22 cm. – (Liberation movement series ; 15)

Contents : v.1. Freedom Struggle – v.2 Freedom struggle – v.3. Freedom movement.

Library lacks vol. 2 (1967)

V44:51 'B47 Libration movement series; 5
K1.1-K 1.3 Tara Chand

The history of freedom movement in India / by Tara Chand; foreword by Humayun Kabir. – Delhi : Publication Division, Govt. of India, 1961-1972.

3 v. ; 22 cm. – (Liberation movement series ; 15)

Contents : v.1. Freedom Struggle – v.2 Freedom struggle– v.3. Freedom movement.

Library lacks vol. 2 (1967)

Personal author
Single author : Indic name

Problem No. 03

Foundations of Modern Psychological Series
Number : 12

NATURE OF PSYCHOLOGICAL INQUIRY

An Analytical Approach

by
Dr. Mohan Sen Gupta

Revised by
Dr. Tanvir Ahmad

Second Revised Edition

WORLD PRESS, Ltd.
Calcutta

1935

- Class No. S:f
- Book No. N 5
- Pages : i-xii and 1-315
- Accession No. 114321
- Size : 23 ½ Centimeter
- The book contains diagrams, charts, graphs, etc.

S:f G 5	Sen Gupta, Mohan
114321	Nature of psychological inquiry : an analytical approach / by Mohan Sen Gupta; revised by Tanvir Ahmad. – 2nd rev. ed. – Calcutta : World Press, 1935. xii, 315 p. : ill, ; 24 cm. – (Foundations of modern psychological series ; 12). 1. Psychology 2. Tanvir Ahmad, rev. 3. Title 4. Series

S:f G 5	PSYCHOLOGY Sen Gupta, Mohan
	Nature of psychological inquiry : an analytical approach / by Mohan Sen Gupta; revised by Tanvir Ahmad. – 2nd rev. ed. – Calcutta : World Press, 1935. xii, 315 p. : ill, ; 24 cm. – (Foundations of modern psychological series ; 12).

S:f G 5	Tanvir Ahmad, *rev.* Sen Gupta, Mohan
	Nature of psychological inquiry : an analytical approach / by Mohan Sen Gupta; revised by Tanvir Ahmad. – 2nd rev. ed. – Calcutta : World Press, 1935. xii, 315 p. : ill, ; 24 cm. – (Foundations of modern psychological series ; 12).

S:f		Nature of psychological inquiry
G 5	Sen Gupta, Mohan	
		Nature of psychological inquiry : an analytical approach / by Mohan Sen Gupta; revised by Tanvir Ahmad. – 2nd rev. ed. – Calcutta : World Press, 1935.
		xii, 315 p. : ill, ; 24 cm. – (Foundations of modern psychological series ; 12).

S:f		Foundations of modern psychological series; 12
G 5	Sen Gupta, Mohan	
		Nature of psychological inquiry : an analytical approach / by Mohan Sen Gupta; revised by Tanvir Ahmad. – 2nd rev. ed. – Calcutta : Word Press, 1935.
		xii, 315 p. : ill, ; 24 cm. – (Foundations of modern psychological series ; 12).

Name Reference Entry

	Gupta, Mohan Sen	
		see Sen Gupta, Mohan

Personal author — Problem No. 04

Single author : Hyphenated name

IRON AND ITS COMPOUNDS

A Manual

by

Prof. Cecil Day — Lewis

Third Edition

Revised by

Dr. Philips Francis

ALLEN & UNWIN Ltd.

London

1955

- Class No. E182
- Book No. J5
- Pages : i-ix and 10-250
- Accession No. 139711
- Size : 27½ x 11½ centimeter
- Contains charts, diagrams, graphs, tables, etc.
- American Chemical Society Scientific Series No. IX

E182 J 5	Day-Lewis, Cecil
139711	Iron and its compounds : a manual / by Cecil Day-Lewis. – 3rd rev. ed. – Revised by Philips Francis. – London: Allen & Unwin, 1955. 250 p. : ill. ; 28 x 12 cm. – American Chemical Society scientific series ; 9). 1. Steel & Iron 2. Francis, Philips, rev. 3. Title 4. Series

E182 J 5	STEEL & IRON Day – Lewis, Cecil
	Iron and its compounds : a manual / by Cecil Day-Lewis. – 3rd rev. ed. – Revised by Philips Francis. – London: Allen & Unwin, 1955. 250 p. : ill. ; 28 x 12 cm. – (American Chemical Society scientific series ; 9).

E182 J 5	Day-Lewis, Cecil	Francis, Philips, rev.
	Day-Lewis. – 3rd rev. ed. – Revised by Philips Francis. – London: Allen & Unwin, 1955. Society scientific series ; 9).	Iron and its compounds : a manual / by Cecil 250 p. : ill. ; 28 x 12 cm. – (American Chemical

E182 J 5	Day-Lewis, Cecil	American Chemical Society scientific series; 9
	Day-Lewis. – 3rd rev. ed. – Revised by Philips Francis. – London: Allen & Unwin, 1955. Society scientific series ; 9).	Iron and its compounds : a manual / by Cecil 250 p. : ill. ; 28 x 12 cm. – (American Chemical

Name Reference Entry

	Lewis, Day-Cecil	
		see Day-Lewis, Cecil

Personal author
Single author

Problem No. 05

VISTAS IN FREE-RADICAL CHEMISTRY

Published
in
Memoriam to Dr. Morris S. Kharasch

Edited by
Dr. William A. Waters

Pergamon Press Limited
London

1959

- Class No. 547.1
- Book No. J9
- Pages: i-ix and 1-251
- Size : 25.50 centimeters
- Accession No. 211321
- International Series of Monographs on Organic Chemistry Vol. 1
- Published in April 1959

547.1 J9	Vistas in free-radical chemistry : published in memoriam to Dr. Morris S. Kharasch / edited by William A. Waters. – London : Pergamon Press, 1959. ix, 251 p. ; 26 cm. – (International series of monographs on organic chemistry ; v. 1) 1. Chemistry, organic. 2. Kharasch, Morris S. 3. Waters, William A., *ed.* 4. Series.

547.1 J9	CHEMISTRY, ORGANIC Vistas in free-radical chemistry : published in memorian to Dr. Morris S. Kharasch / edited by William A. Waters. – London : Pergamon Press, 1959. ix, 251 p. ; 26 cm. – (International series of monographs on organic chemistry ; v. 1)

547.1 KHARASCH, MORRIS S.
J9 Vistas in free-radical chemistry : published in memoriam to Dr. Morris S. Kharasch / edited by William A.Waters. – London : Pergamon Press, 1959.

ix, 251 p. ; 26 cm. – (International series of monographs on organic chemistry ; v. 1)

547.1 Waters, William A., *ed.*
J9 Vistas in free-radical chemistry : published in memoriam to Dr. Morris S. Kharasch / edited by William A. Waters. – London : Pergamon Press, 1959.

ix, 251 p. ; 26 cm. – (International series of monographs on organic chemistry ; v. 1)

547.1 International series of monographs on organic...
J9 Vistas in free-radical chemistry: published in memoriam to Dr. Morris S. Kharasch / edited by William A. Waters. – London : Pergamon Press, 1959.

ix, 251 p. ; 26 cm. – (International series of monographs on organic chemistry ; v. 1)

Personal Author Problem No. 6
Single : Author Arden Edition

THE MERCHANT OF VENICE

Edited by
Prof. Horace Howard Furness

Fifth Edition

METHEUN AND COMPANY LTD.
London

1955

- Class No. 0111,2J64,4
- Book No. J5
- Pages : i-x and 1-351
- Accession No. 122112
- From Half Title-page: Arden Edition of the Works of William Shakespear, item : 9 of Arden
- Size : 21 ½ x 12 ½ centimeter

0111,2J64,4
J 5

Shakespeare, William

The merchant of Venice / [by William Shakespere] ; edited by Horace Howard Furness. – 5th ed., Arden ed. – London: Methuen, 1955.

x, 351 p. ; 21 x 13 cm. – (Works of William Shakespeare, 1943, Arden ed. ; 9)

122112

1. English literature 2. Furness, Horace Howard, ed. 3. Title 4. Series

---

0111,2J64,4
J5

ENGLISH LITERATURE
Shakespeare, William

The merchant of Venice / [by William Shakespere] ; edited by Horace Howard Furness. – 5th ed., Arden ed.—London: Methuen, 1955.

x, 351 p. ; 21 x 13 cm. – (Works of William Shakespeare, 1943, Arden ed. ; 9)

0111,2J64,4 J 5		Furness, Horace Howard, *ed.* Shakespeare, William
		The merchant of Venice / [by William Shakespere] ; edited by Horace Howard Furness. – 5th ed., Arden ed. — London: Methuen, 1955. x, 351 p. ; 21 x 13 cm. – (Works of William Shakespeare, 1943, Arden ed.; 9)

0111,2J64,4 J 5		The Merchant of Venice Shakespeare, William
		The merchant of Venice / [by William Shakespere] ; edited by Horace Howard Furness. – 5th ed., Arden ed.— London: Methuen, 1953. x, 351 p. ; 21 x 13 cm. – (Works of William Shakespeare, 1943, Arden ed.; 9)

0111,2J64,4 J 5		Works of William Shakespeare, 1943 Arden ed.; 9 Shakespeare, William
		The merchant of Venice / [by William Shakespere] ; edited by Horace Howard Furness. – 5th ed., Arden ed. — London: Methuen, 1955. x, 351 p. ; 21 x 13 cm. – (Works of William Shakespeare, 1943, Arden ed.; 9)

Personal Author Problem No. 7

Single Author : Author's Name Merged

SAYERS' MANUAL
OF
CLASSIFICATION FOR LIBRARIES

Fifth Edition

By
Arthur Maltby

Andre Deutsch / A Grafton Book
London

1975

- Class No. 025.4
- Book No. L5
- Pages : i-x & 1-336
- Accession No. 112412
- size : 21 ½ centimeters
- Originally published by Williams Charles Berwick Sayers (1881-1960) in 1926 under title "A Manual of Classification".
- Third Edition was published under title : A Manual for Librarians and Bibliographers
- Fourth Edition was published under title : A Manual of Classification for Librarians, completely revised and partly re-written by Arthur Maltby in 1975.

025.4
L 5

Sayers, William Charles Berwick, 1881-1960

Sayers's manual of classification for libraries. – 5th ed. / by Arthur Maltby. – London : Andre Deutsch, 1975.

v, 336 p. ; 22 cm. – (A Grafton book).

Originally published in 1926 under title : A manual of classification.

3rd ed. published under title : A manual for librarians and bibliographers

4th ed. published under title : A manual classification for librarians completely rev. and partly re-written by Arthur Maltby.

(Continued on next card)

Continued Card

025.4
L 5

Sayers, William Charles Berwick, 1881-1960

Sayers's manual of classification for librarians of 1975. (Card 2).

1. Classification – libraries 2. Maltby Arthur, *rev.* 3. Title

025.4	CLASSIFICATION – LIBRARIES
L 5	Sayers, William Charles Berwick, 1881-1960
	Sayers's manual of classification for libraries. – 5th ed. / by Arthur Maltby. – London : Andre Deutsch, 1975.
	v, 336 p. ; 22 cm. – (A Grafon book).
	Originally published in 1926 under title A manual of classification.
	3rd ed. published under title : A manual for librarians and bibliographers.
	4th ed. published under title : A manual of classification for librarians completely – rev. and partly re-written by Arthur Maltby.

025.4	Maltby, Arthur, *rev.*
L 5	Sayers, William Charles Berwick, 1881-1960
	Sayers's manual of classification for libraries. – 5th ed. / by Arthur Maltby. – London : Andre Deutsch, 1975.
	v, 336 p. ; 22 cm. – (A Grafon book).
	Originally published in 1926 under title A manual of classification.
	3rd ed. published under title : A manual for librarians and bibliographers.
	4th ed. published under title : A manual of classification for librarians completely – rev. and partly re-written by Arthur Maltby.

025.4 L 5	Sayer's manual of classification for libraries Sayers, William Charles Berwick, 1881-1960.
	Sayers's manual of classification for libraries. – 5th ed. / by Arthur Maltby. – London : Andre Deutsch, 1975. v, 336 p. ; 22 cm. – (A Grafon book). Originally published in 1926 under title A manual of classification. 3rd ed. published under title : A manual for librarians and bibliographers. 4th ed. published under title : A manual of classification for librarians completely – rev. and partly re-written by Arthur Maltby.

Personal Author Problem No. 8

Two Author and Editor

THE
ANALYTICAL STUDY
OF
INDUSTRIAL RELATIONS

A Human Aspect of Administration

by
Prof. Ehsan Ali
and
Dr. Rizwan Ahmad Ansari

Third Revised Edition

Revised by
Dr. Vijay Kumar Misra

Osmania University Southern
Regional Centre
Hyderabad

1957

- X:97
- Book No. J 7
- Accession No. 132314
- Size : 24½ centimeters
- Osmania University Personnel Management and Human Relations Series No. XXI
- Pages : i-v and 6-395

X:97 J 7	Ehsan Ali	
132314	The analytical study of industrial relations : a human aspect of administration / by Ehsan Ali and Rizwan Ahmad Ansari. – 3rd rev. ed. – Revised by Vijay Kumar Misra. – Hyderabad : Osmania Uny. Southern Regional Centre, 1957. 395 p. ; 25 cm. – (Osmania Uny. Personnel management and human relation series ; 21). 1. Personnel management 2. Ansari, Rizwan Ahmad 3. Misra, Vijay Kumar, rev. 4. Title. 5. Series	

X:97 J 7	PERSONNEL MANAGEMENT Ehsan Ali	
	The analytical study of industrial relations : a human aspect of administration / by Ehsan Ali and Rizwan Ahmad Ansari. – 3rd rev. ed. – Revised by Vijay Kumar Misra. – Hyderabad : Osmania Uny. Southern Regional Centre, 1957 395 p.; 25 cm. – (Osmania Uny. Personnel management and human relations series ; 21).	

X:97 J 7		Ansari, Rizwan Ahmad Ehsan Ali
		The analytical study of industrial relations : a human aspect of administration / by Ehsan Ali and Rizwan Ahmad Ansari. – 3rd rev. ed. – Revised by Vijay Kumar Misra. – Hyderabad : Osmania Uny. Southern Regional Centre, 1957 395 p.; 25 cm. – (Osmania Uny. Personnel management and human relations series ; 21).

X:97 J 7		Misra, Vijay Kumar, rev. Ehsan Ali
		The analytical study of industrial relations : a human aspect of administration / by Ehsan Ali and Rizwan Ahmad Ansari. – 3rd rev. ed. – Revised by Vijay Kumar Misra. – Hyderabad : Osmania Uny. Southern Regional Centre, 1957 395 p.; 25 cm. – (Osmania Uny. Personnel management and human relations series ; 21).

X:97 J 7		The Analytical study of industrial relations Ehsan Ali
		The analytical study of industrial relations : a human aspect of administration / by Ehsan Ali and Rizwan Ahmad Ansari. – 3rd rev. ed. – Revised by Vijay Kumar Misra. – Hyderabad : Osmania Uny. Southern Regional Centre, 1957, 395 p. ; 25 cm. – (Osmania Univ. Personnel management and human relation series ; 21). ○

X:97 J 7		Osmania Univ. Personnel management and …; 21 Ehsan Ali
		The analytical study of industrial relations : a human aspect of administration / by Ehsan Ali and Rizwan Ahmad Ansari. – 3rd rev. ed. – Revised by Vijay Kumar Misra. – Hyderabad : Osmania Uny. Southern Regional Centre, 1957, 395 p. ; 25 cm. – (Osmania Univ. Personnel management and human relation series ; 21). ○

Personal Author
Two author

Problem No. 9

THE RURAL DEVELOPMENT IN INDIA

Theories of Peasant Economy
and
Agrarian Change

by

Prof. Iqbal Ahmad
and
Dr. Roshan Lal

Third Revised Edition

SAGAR PUBLICATION HOUSE
Coimbatore

1982

- Class No. Y31:7.44
- Book No. M 2
- Size : 24½ centimeters
- New Landmarks of Rural and Agrarian Development Series No. IX
- Size : 24½ centimeters
- Accession No. 213412
- Pages : i-v and 1-312

Y31:7.44
M 2 Iqbal Ahmad

The rural development in India : theories of peasant economy and agrarian change / by Iqbal Ahmad and Roshan Lal. – 3rd rev. ed. – Coimbatore : Sagar Publication House, 1982.

213412 v, 312 p. ; 25 cm. – (New Land marks of rural and agrarian development series; 9).

1. Peasant economy 2. Rural development 3. Roshan Lal 4. Title 5. Series

---

Y31:7.44 RURAL DEVELOPMENT
M 2 Iqbal Ahmad

The rural development in India : theories of peasant economy and agrarian change / by Iqbal Ahmad and Roshan Lal. – 3rd rev. ed. – Coimbatore : Sagar Publication House, 1982.

v, 312 p. ; 25 cm. – (New landmarks of rural and agrarian development series ; 9).

Y31:7.44 PEASANT ECONOMY
M 2 Iqbal Ahmad

The rural development in India : theories of peasant economy and agrarian change / by Iqbal Ahmad and Roshan Lal. – 3rd rev. ed. – Coimbatore : Sagar Publication House, 1982.

v, 312 p. ; 25 cm. – (New landmarks of rural and agrarian development series ; 9).

Y31:7.44		Roshan Lal
M2	Iqbal	Ahmad
		The rural development in India : theories of peasant economy and agrarian change / by Iqbal Ahmad and Roshan Lal. – 3rd rev. ed. – Coimbatore : Sagar Publication House, 1982.
		v, 312 p. ; 25 cm. – (New landmarks of rural and agrarian development series ; 9).

Y31:7.44		The Rural development in India
M2	Iqbal	Ahmad
		The rural development in India : theories of peasant economy and agrarian change / by Iqbal Ahmad and Roshan Lal. – 3rd rev. ed. – Coimbatore : Sagar Publication House, 1982.
		v, 312 p. ; 25 cm. – (New landmarks of rural and agrarian development series; 9).

Y31:7.44		New landmarks of rural and agrarian ...
M 2	Iqbal	Ahmad
		The rural development in India : theories of peasant economy and agrarian change / by Iqbal Ahmad and Roshan Lal. – 3rd rev. ed. – Coimbatore : Sagar Publication House, 1982.
		v, 312 p. ; 25 cm. – (New landmarks of rural and agrarian development series ; 9).

Personal Author Problem No. 10
Two Author and Multi-volumed Book

INDUSTRIAL IMPACT
ON
INDIAN SOCIETY

by
Dr. Ram Kumar
and
Dr. Bimal K. Chatterjee

(In Three Volumes)

METROPOLITAN BOOK CO. Ltd.
Delhi — Bombay

1967

- Class No. Y744&gXB(A)
- Book No. K7.1 – K7.3
- Size : 24½ X 12¼ centimeters
- Accession Nos. 14356, 14357 and 14358
- Science and Industrial Development Series No. XVI

Y744&gXB(A) K7.1-K7.3	Ram Kumar
1435658	Industrial impact on Indian society / by Ram Kumar and Bimal K. Chatterjee. – Calcutta : Metropolitan Books, 1967. 3 v. : ill.; 24 cm. – (Science and industrial development series ; 16) 1. Industry 2. Social change 3. Chatterjee, Bimal K. 4. Title 5. Series

Y744&gXB(A) K7.1-K7.3	INDUSTRY Ram Kumar
	Industrial impact on Indian society / by Ram Kumar and Bimal K. Chatterjee. – Calcutta : Metropolitan Books, 1967. 3 v. : ill. ; 24 cm. – (Science and industrial development series ; 16)

Y744&gXB(A) K7.1-K7.3	SOCIAL CHANGE Ram Kumar
	Industrial impact on Indian society / by Ram Kumar and Bimal K. Chatterjee. – Calcutta : Metropolitan Books, 1967. 3 v. : ill. ; 24 cm. – (Science and industrial development series ; 16)

Y744&gXB(A)
K7.1-K7.3

Chaterjee, Bimal K.

Ram Kumar

Industrial impact on Indian society / by Ram Kumar and Bimal K. Chatterjee. – Calcutta : Metropolitan Books, 1967.

3v. : ill. ; 24 cm. – (Science and industrial development series ; 16)

Y744&gXB(A)
K7.1-K7.3

Industrial impact on Indian society

Ram Kumar

Industrial impact on Indian society / by Ram Kumar and Bimal K. Chatterjee. – Calcutta : Metropolitan Books, 1967.

3v. : ill. ; 24 cm. – (Science and industrial development series ; 16)

Y744&gXB(A)
K7.1-K7.3

Science and industrial development series; 16

Ram Kumar

Industrial impact on Indian society / by Ram Kumar and Bimal K. Chatterjee. – Calcutta : Metropolitan Books, 1967.

3v. : ill. ; 24 cm. – (Science and industrial development series ; 16)

Personal Author
Three Authors

Problem No. 11

Samuel W. Bloom
Daniel H. Calhoun
GEORGE H. MARSHAL

THE DOCTOR AND HIS PATIENT

Third Edition

ALAN ROSS & Company Ltd.
30, Thurloe Place
LONDON, S.W. 7

- Class No. 610.696
- Book No. K5
- Russel Sage Publications in Medical Science No. VI
- Copyright May 1963
- Pages: i-vii and 1-268
- First edition 1962; Second edition 1969; Third edition 1985
- Accession No. 121102
- Size : 28.25 x 10.25 centimeters

610.696 K 5	Marshal, George H.
	The doctor and his patient / Samuel W. Bloom, Daniel H. Calhoun and George H. Marshal. – 3rd ed. – London : Alan Ross, 1985c.
121102	vii, 268 p. ; 29 x 11 cm. – (Russel Sage Publications in medical science ; 6)
	1. Medical treatment 2. Bloom, Samuel W. 3.Calhoun, Daniel H. 4. Title 5. Series.

610.696 K 5	MEDICAL TREATMENT Marshal, George H.
	The doctor and his patient / Samuel W. Bloom, Daniel H. Calhoun and George H. Marshal. – 3rd ed. – London : Alan Ross, 1985c.
	vii, 268 p. ; 29 x 11 cm. – (Russel Sage Publications in medical science ; 6)

610.696 K 5	Bloom, Samuel W. Marshal, George H.
	The doctor and his patient / Samuel W. Bloom, Daniel H. Calhoun and George H. Marshal. – 3rd ed. – London : Alan Ross, 1985c.
	vii, 268 p. ; 29 x 11 cm. – (Russel Sage Publications in medical science ; 6)

610.696 K 5	Calhoun, Daniel H. Marshal, George H.
	The doctor and his patient / Samuel W. Bloom, Daniel H. Calhoun and George H. Marshal. – 3rd ed. – London : Alan Ross, 1985c. vii, 268 p. ; 29 x 11 cm. – (Russel Sage publications in medical science ; 6)

610.696 K 5	The Doctor and his patient Marshal, George H.
	The doctor and his patient / Samuel W. Bloom, Daniel H. Calhoun and George H. Marshal. – 3rd ed. – London : Alan Ross, 1985c. vii, 268 p. ; 29 x 11 cm. – (Russel Sage publications in medical science ; 6)

610.696 K 5	Russel Sage publication in medical science; 6 Marshal, George H.
	The doctor and his patient / Samuel W. Bloom, Daniel H. Calhoun and George H. Marshal. – 3rd ed. – London : Alan Ross, 1985. vii, 268 p. ; 29 x 11 cm. – (Russel Sage publications in medical science ; 6)

Personal Author Problem No. 12
Three Authors

THERAPEUTICS
of
NERVE DISEASES

An Objective
and
Analytical Approach

by
Dr. Harry S. Gear
Dr. George H. Marshal
and
Dr. Maurice W. Goldsmith

RICHARD PETERSON Ltd.
LONDON

1987

- Class No. L74:4:6
- Book No. M 7
- Pages : i-v and 1-241
- Accession No. 112211
- New Monographic Series on Nervous System Number XXI
- The book contains diagrams, charts, graphs, tables, etc.
- Size : 25¼ x 10¼ centimeters

L74:4:6 M 7	Gear, Harry S.	
112211	Therapeutics of nerve diseases : an objective and analytical approach / by Harry S. Gear, George H. Marshal and Maurice W. Goldsmith. – 4th rev. ed. – London : Richard Peterson, 1987. v, 241 p. : ill. ; 26 x 11 cm. – (New monographic series on nervous system ; 21). 1. Therapy – nervous system. 2. Marshal George H. 3. Goldsmith, Maurice W 4. Title 5. Series	

L74:4:6 M 7	THERAPY – NERVOUS SYSTEM Gear, Harry S.	
	Therapeutics of nerve diseases : an objective and analytical approach / by Harry S. Gear, George H. Marshal and Maurice W. Goldsmith. – 4th rev. ed. – London : Richard Paterson, 1987. v, 241 p. : ill. ; 26 x 11 cm. – (New monographic series on nervous system ; 21).	

L74:4:6 M 7	Marshal, George H. Gear, Harry S.	
	Therapeutics of nerve diseases : an objective and analytical approach / by Harry S. Gear, George H. Marshal and Maurice W. Goldsmith. – 4th rev. ed. – London : Richard Peterson, 1987. v, 241 p. : ill. ; 26 x 11 cm. – (New monographic series on nervous system ; 21).	

L74:4:6 M 7		Goldsmith, Maurice W. Gear, Harry S.
		Therapeutics of nerve diseases : an objective and analytical approach / by Harry S. Gear, George H. Marshal and Maurice W. Goldsmith. – 4th rev. ed. – London : Richard Peterson, 1987. v, 241 p. : ill. ; 26 x 11 cm. – (New monographic series on nervous system ; 21).

L74:4:6 M 7		Therapeutics of nerve diseases Gear, Harry S.
		Therapeutics of nerve diseases : an objective and analytical approach / by Harry S. Gear, George H. Marshal and Maurice W. Goldsmith. – 4th rev. ed. – London : Richard Peterson, 1987. v, 241 p. : ill. ; 26 x 11 cm. – (New monographic series on nervous system ; 21).

L74:4:6 M 7		New monographic series on nervous ... Gear, Harry S.
		Therapeutics of nerve diseases : an objective and analytical approach / by Harry S. Gear, George H. Marshal and Maurice W. Goldsmith. – 4th rev. ed. – London : Richard Peterson, 1987. v, 241 p. : ill. ; 26 x 11 cm. – (New monographic series on nervous system ; 21).

Personal Author Problem No. 13
Three author and Collaborators

RESEARCH METHODS
IN
SOCIAL RELATIONS

CLAIRE SELLTIZ
LAWRENCE S. WRIGHTSMAN
STUART W. COOK

in collaboration with

George J. Balch
Richard Hafsteller
&
Leonard Bickman

HOLT, RINEHART & WINSTON
New York

1976

- Class No. 301.018
- Book No. L 6
- Pages : i-v and 1-624
- Size : 23.15 centimeters
- Accession No. 122431

301.018 L 6	Selltiz, Claire
122431	Research methods in social relations / Claire Sellit Lawrence S. Wrightsman Stauart W. Cook in collaboration with George J. Balch, Richard Hafsteller and Leonard Bickman. – New York : Holt, Rinehart and Winston, 1976. xv, 624 p. ; 24 cm. 1. Sociology-Research 2. Wrightsman, Lawrence S. 3. Cook, Staurt W. 4. Title

301.018 L 6	SOCIOLOGY – RESEARCH Selltiz, Claire
	Research methods in social relations / Claire Sellit Lawrence S. Wrightsman Stauart W. Cook in collaboration with George J. Balch, Richard Hafsteller & Leonard Bickman. – New York : Holt, Rinehart and Winston, 1976. xv, 624 p. ; 24 cm.

301.015 L 6	Wrightsman Stauart, S. Selltiz, Claire
	Research methods in social relations / Claire Sellit Lawrence S. Wrightsman Stauart W. Cook in collaboration with George J. Balch, Richard Hafsteller and Leonard Bickman. – New York : Holt, Rinehart and Winston, 1976. v, 624 p. ; 24 cm.

301.015 Cook, Staurt W.
L 6 Selltiz, Claire

Research methods in social relations / Claire Sellit Lawrence S. Wrightsman Stauart W. Cook in collaboration with George J. Balch, Richard Hafsteller and Leonard Bickman. – New York : Holt, Rinehart and Winston, 1976.

v, 624 p. ; 24 cm.

301.015 Methods in social relations
L 6 Selltiz, Claire

Research methods in social relations / Claire Sellit Lawrence S. Wrightsman Stauart W. Cook in collaboration with George J. Balch, Richard Hafsteller and Leonard Bickman. – New York : Holt, Rinehart and Winston, 1976.

v, 624 p. ; 24 cm.

Personal Author Problem No. 14
Four Author – No Principal Author

PHILOSOPHY OF PHYSICAL EDUCATION

A Study of
Social Matrix
&
Sports

by
Dr. Kartar Singh Grewal
Dr. Surendra Singh Ahuja
Dr. Rajesh Charan Gautam
and
Dr. Sita Ram Sharma

Second Edition

Oriental Publication House Ltd.
Jaipur

1969

- Class No. T : 6
- Book No. K 9
- Pages : i-ix and 10-395
- Size : 23½ Centimeters
- Golden Series in Physical Education and Sports Number : XII
- Accession No. 116913

T : 6
K 9

Philosophy of physical education : a study of social matrix & sports / by Kartar Singh Grewal ... [et al.] . – 2nd ed. – Jaipur : Oriental Publication House, 1969.

116913

395 p. ; 24 cm. – (Golden series in physical education and sports ; 12).

1. Physical education 2. Sports education 3. Grewal, Kartar Singh 4. Series

---

T : 6
K 9

PHYSICAL EDUCATION

Philosophy of physical education : a study of social matrix & sports / by Kartar Singh Grewal ... [et al.] . – 2nd ed. – Jaipur : Oriental Publication House, 1969.

395 p. ; 24 cm. – (Golden series in physical education and sports ; 12).

T:6
K 9

SPORTS EDUCATION

Philosophy of physical education : a study of social matrix & sports / by Kartar Singh Grewal ... [et al.] . – 2nd ed. – Jaipur : Oriental Publication House, 1969.

395 p. ; 24 cm. – (Golden series in physical education and sports ; 12).

T:6
K 9

Grewal, Kartar Singh

Philosophy of physical education : a study of social matrix & sports / by Kartar Singh Grewal ... [et al.] .— 2nd ed. – Jaipur : Oriental Publication House, 1969.

395 p. ; 24 cm. – (Golden series in physical education and sports ; 12).

T:6
K 9

Golden series in physical education and ...

Philosophy of physical education : a study of social matrix & sports / by Kartar Singh Grewal ... [et al.] . – 2nd ed. – Jaipur : Oriental Publication House, 1969.

395 p. ; 24 cm. – (Golden series in physical education and sports ; 12).

Personal Author Problem No. 15
Four Author – Principal Author Indicated

FUNDAMENTALS OF CHEMOTHERAPY

by
Prof. Ranjan P. Mathur
Prof. PREM NATH
Dr. Gyan Kumar Rastogi
and
Dr. Raj Narain Misra

Third Revised Edition

Revised by
Dr. Hans Kumar Chopra

MODERN PUBLISHERS Ltd.
Delhi – Bhopal - Kolkata

1989

- Class No. L: 4: 6(E)
- Book No. M 9
- Accession No. 212397
- Size : 22¼ Centimeters
- Pages : i-xii and 1-463
- Modern Medical Publication Series No. VI
- The book contains photo-plates, diagrams, charts, graphs, tables, etc.

L:4:6(E) M 9	Prem Nath
212397	Fundamentals of chemotherapy / by Ranjan P. Mathur ... [et al.] – 3rd rev. ed. – Revised by Hans Kumar Chopra. – Delhi : Modern Publishers, 1989. xii, 463 p. : ill. ; 23 cm. – (Modern medical publication series ; 6) 1. Therapeutics 2. Mathur, Ranjan P. 3. Chopra, Hans Kumar, *rev.* 4. Title 5. Series.

Note : Whenever the number of authors of a book exceeds three (3), mention in the statement of responsibility the first-named author giving three dots ... to show the omission of remaining authors, mentioning within square brackets [et al.] as prescribed in AACR – II rule No. 2.1F1.

L:4:6(E) M 9	THERAPEUTICS Prem Nath
	Fundamentals of chemotherapy / by Ranjan P. Mathur ... [et al.] – 3rd rev. ed. – Revised by Hans Kumar Chopra. – Delhi : Modern Publishers, 1989. xii, 463 p. : ill. ; 23 cm. – (Modern medical publication series ; 6)

L:4:6(E) M 9	Chopra, Hans Kumar, *rev.* Prem Nath
	Fundamentals of chemotherapy / by Ranjan P. Mathur ... [et al.] – 3rd rev. ed. – Revised by Hans Kumar Chopra. – Delhi : Modern Publishers, 1989. xii, 463 p. : ill. ; 23 cm. – (Modern medical publication series ; 6)

L:4:6(E) M 9	Prem Nath	Fundamentals of chemotherapy
		Fundamentals of chemotherapy / by Ranjan P. Mathur ... [et al.] – 3rd rev. ed. – Revised by Hans Kumar Chopra. – Delhi : Modern Publishers, 1989. xii, 463 p. : ill. ; 23 cm. – (Modern medical publication series ; 6)

L:4:6(E) M 9	Prem Nath	Modern medical publication series; 6
		Fundamentals of chemotherapy / by Ranjan P. Mathur ... [et al.] – 3rd rev. ed. – Revised by Hans Kumar Chopra. – Delhi : Modern Publishers, 1989. xii, 463 p. : ill. ; 23 cm. – (Modern medical publication series ; 6)

L:4:6(E) M 9	Prem Nath	Mathur, Ranjan P.
		Fundamentals of chemotherapy / by Ranjan P. Mathur ... [et al.] – 3rd rev. ed. – Revised by Hans Kumar Chopra. – Delhi : Modern Publishers, 1989. xii, 463 p. : ill. ; 23 cm. – (Modern medical publication series ; 6)

Dictionaries with Editor & Reviser | Problem No. 16

CASSELL'S NEW ENGLISH DICTIONARY

Edited by
Ernest A. Baker

Revised and Enlarged

by
Arthur L. Hayward

Cassells and Co. Ltd.
London – Toronto

1979

- Class No. 423
- Book No. L 9
- Pages : i-xii and 1682
- Contains pictures, charts, diagrams tables, sketches, etc.
- Accession No. 212397
- Size : 28 ½ Centimeters

423
L 9 Cassell's New English dictionary / edited by Ernest A. Baker ; revised and enlarged by Arthur L. Hayward. – London ; Toronto : Cassell, 1979.

212397 xiii, 1682 p. : ill. ; 29 cm.

1. English – dictionaries. 2. Baker, Ernest A., ed. 3. Hayward, Arthur L., *rev.*

---

423 ENGLISH – DICTIONARIES
L 9 Cassell's New English dictionary / edited by Ernest A. Baker ; revised and enlarged by Arthur L. Hayward. – London ; Toronto : Cassell, 1979.

xiii, 1682 p. : ill. ; 29 cm.

423		Baker, Ernest A., ed.
L 9		Cassell's new English dictionary / edited by Ernest A. Baker ; revised and enlarged by Arthur L. Hayward. – London ; Toronto : Cassell, 1979.
		xiii, 1682 p. : ill. ; 29 cm.

423		Hayward, Arthur L., rev.
L 9		Cassell's New English dictionary / edited by Ernest A. Baker ; revised and enlarged by Arthur L. Hayward. – London ; Toronto : Cassell, 1979.
		xiii, 1682 p. : ill. ; 29 cm.

Encyclopedias Problem No. 17

VAN NOSTRAND's SCIENTIFIC ENCYCLOPEDIA

Fifth Revised Edition

Edited by
Douglas M. Considine

VAN NOSTRAND REINHOLD, Inc.
New York

1976

- Class No. Ak
- Book No. L 6
- Accession No. 122431
- Pages : i-xiii and 1-761
- Size : 27 ¼ Centimeters

Ak L 6	Van Nostrand's scientific encyclopedia / edited by	
	Douglas M. considine. – 5th rev. ed. – New York : Van Nostrand Reinhold, 1976. xiii, 761 p. : ill. ; 28 cm.	
122431	1. Science – encyclopedia. 2. Considine, Douglas M., ed.	

Ak L 6	SCIENCE – ENCYCLOPEDIA Van Nostrand's scientific encyclopedia / edited by	
	Douglas M. Considine. – 5th rev. ed. – New York : Van Nostrand Reinhold, 1976. xiii, 761 p. : ill. ; 28 cm.	

Ak L 6	Considine, Douglas M., ed. Van Nostrand's scientific encyclopedia / edited by	
	Douglas M. Considine. – 5th rev. ed. – New York : Van Nostrand Reinhold, 1976. xiii, 761 p. : ill. ; 28 cm.	

Editorial Work Problem No. 18
Two Editors

STUDIES
IN
APPLIED PHYSICS

Edited by
Dr. Rex C. Swits
and
Dr. Smith T. Crompton

Third Enlarged Edition

Little Brown & Co. Ltd.
LONDON

1947

- Class No. C
- Book No. H 7
- Pages : i-ix and 1-356
- Accession No. 145910
- The book contains graphs, diagrams, charts, photos etc.

C
H 7 Studies in applied physics / edited by Rex C. Swits and Smith T. Crompton. – 3rd enl. ed. – London: Little Brown, 1947.

ix, 356 p. : ill. ; 22 cm.

145910 1. Applied physics 2. Swits, Rex C., ed. 3. Crompton, Smith T., jt. ed.

C APPLIED PHYSICS
H 7 Studies in applied physics / edited by Rex C. Swits and Smith T. Crompton. – 3rd enl. ed. – London: Little Brown, 1947.

ix, 356 p. : ill. ; 22 cm.

C Swits, Rex C., ed.
H 7 Studies in applied physics / edited by Rex C. Swits and Smith T. Crompton. – 3rd enl. ed. – London: Little Brown, 1947.

ix, 356 p. : ill. ; 22 cm.

C Crompton, Smith T., jt. ed.
H 7 Studies in applied physics / edited by Rex C. Swits and Smith T. Crompton. – 3rd enl. ed. – London: Little Brown, 1947.

ix, 356 p. : ill. ; 22 cm.

Editorial Work Problem No. 19
Multi-Volumed Book

A COURSE OF
HIGHER MATHEMATICS

Edited by
Dr. I.N. Sneddon

Translated by Dr. D.E. Brown

(In 5 Volumes)

Pergamon Press, Inc.,
New York

1964

- Class No. 510.8
- Book No. K 4.1 – K4.5
- Size : 21¼ centimeters
- The book contains diagrammatic equations, graphs, charts, tables, etc.
- Contents : Vol. 1 : Elementary Calculas
  Vol. 2 : Advance Calculas
  Vol. 3 : Part - 1 : Linear Algebra
  Part - 2 : Complex Variable
  Special Function
  Vol. 4 : Integral Equation and Partial Equation
  Vol. 5 : Integral and Functional Analysis
- Accession Nos. 132124, 132125, 132126, 132127 and 132128

510.8
K4.1-K4.5 A course of higher mathematics / edited by I.N. Sneddon; translated by D.E. Brown. – New York : Pergamon Press, 1964.

5 v. : ill. ; 22 cm.

Contents : v. 1. Elementary calculus – v. 2. Advance calculus – v. 3 pt. 1. Linear algebra – v. 3. pt. 2. Complex variable special function – v. 4. Integral equation and partial equation – v. 5 Integral and functional analysis.

132124-28 1. Calculas 2. Higher algebra 3. Complex variable 4. Integral function 5. Sneddon, I.N., ed. 6. Brown, D.E., tr.

510.8 CALCULAS
K4.1-K4.5 A course of higher mathematics / edited by I.N. Sneddon; translated by D.E. Brown. – New York : Pergamon Press, 1964

5 v. : ill. ; 22 cm.

Contents : v.1 . Elementary calculus – v. 2. Advance calculus – v. 3 pt. 1. Linear algebra – v. 3. pt. 2. Complex variable special function – v. 4. Integrated equation and partial equation – 5. Integral and functional analysis.

510.8
K4.1-K4.5

HIGHER ALGEBRA

A course of higher mathematics / edited by I.N. Sneddon; translated by D.E. Brown. – New York : Pergamon Press, 1964.

5 v. : ill. ; 22 cm.

Contents : v. 1. Elementary calculus – v. 2. Advance calculus – v. 3 pt. 1. Linear algebra – v. 3. pt. 2. Complex variable special function – v.4. Integral equation and partial equation – v. 5. Integral and functional analysis.

510.8
K4.1-K4.5

COMPLEX VARIABLE

A course of higher mathematics / edited by I.N. Sneddon; translated by D.E. Brown. – New York : Pergamon Press, 1964

5 v. : ill. ; 22 cm.

Contents : v. 1. Elementary calculus – v. 2. Advance calculus – v. 3 pt. 1. Linear algebra – v. 3. pt. 2. Complex variable special function – v.4. Integral equation and partial equation – v. 5. Integral and functional analysis.

510.8
K4.1-K4.5

INTEGRAL FUNCTION

A course of higher mathematics / edited by I.N. Sneddon, translated by D.E. Brown. – New York : Pergamon Press, 1964.

5 v. : ill. ; 22 cm.

Contents : v. 1. Elementary calculus – v. 2. Advance calculus – v. 3 pt. 1. Linear algebra – v. 3. pt. 2. Complex variable special function – v.4. Integral equation and partial equation – v. 5. Integral and functional analysis.

510.8
K4.1-K4.5

Sneddon, I.N., ed.

A course of higher mathematics / edited by I.N. Sneddon, translated by D.E. Brown. – New York : Pergamon Press, 1964

5 v. : ill. ; 22 cm.

Contents : v. 1. Elementary calculus – v. 2. Advance calculus – v. 3 pt. 1. Linear algebra – v. 3. pt. 2. Complex variable special function – v.4. Integral equation and partial equation – v. 5. Integral and functional analysis.

510.8
K4.1-K4.5

Brown, D.E., tr.

A course of higher mathematics / edit. Edited by I.N. Sneddon; translated by D.E. Brown. – New York : Pergamon Press, 1964.

5 v. : ill. ; 22 cm.

Contents : v. 1. Elementary calculus – v. 2. Advance calculus – v. 3 pt.1. Linear algebra – v. 3. pt. 2. Complex variable special function v. 4. Integral equation and partial equation – v. 5. Integral and functional analysis.

Sacred Scriptures
Bible

Problem No. 20

HOLY BIBLE
Old and New Testaments

Oxford University Press
London

1866

- Class No. 220
- Book No. A66
- Accession No. 156841
- Size : 21½ centimeters
- Pages : Various paging

220 A 66	Bible	*OT & NT. English.*
		Holy Bible : old and new testaments. – London : Oxford University Press, 1866. Various paging. ; 22 cm.
m156841		1. Religion – Christianity. 2. Title

220		RELIGION — CHRISTIANITY
K 66	Bible	*OT & NT. English.*
		Holy Bible : old and new testaments. – London : Oxford University Press, 1866. Various paging. ; 22 cm.

220		Holy Bible
A 66	Bible	*OT & NT. English.*
		Holy Bible : old and new testaments. – London : Oxford University Press, 1866. Various paging. ; 22 cm.

Sacred Scriptures Problem No. 21
Gita

THE BHAGAVAD GITA

Translated by
JUAN MASCARO

PENGUIN BOOKS
Baltimore (Maryland)

1962

- Class No. R68,6
- Book No. K2
- Pages : i-v and 1-121
- Accession No. 124561
- The Penguin classics No. 120
- The book is in English language

R68,6 K 2	Mahabharata. *Bhagavatgita. English.*
124561	The Bhagavad gita / translated by Juan Mascaro. – Baltimore : Penguin, 1962. v, 121 p. ; 18 cm. – (The Penguin Classics ; 120) 1. Indian philosophy. 2. Mascara, Juan, tr. 3. Series

R68,6 K 2	INDIAN — PHILOSOPHY Mahabharata. *Bhagavatgita. English.*
	The Bhagavad gita / translated by Juan Mascaro. – Baltimore : Penguin, 1962. v, 121 p. ; 18 cm. – (The Penguin Classics ; 120)

R68,6 K 2	Mascaro, Juan, *tr.* Mahabharata. *Bhagavatgita. English.*
	The Bhagavad gita / translated by Juan Mascaro. – Baltimore : Penguin, 1962. v, 121 p. ; 18 cm. – (The Penguin Classics ; 120)

R68,6 K 2	The Penguin Classics; 120 Mahabharata. *Bhagavatgita. English.*
	The Bhagavad gita / translated by Juan Mascaro. – Baltimore : Penguin, 1962. v, 121 p. ; 18 cm. – (The Penguin Classics ; 120)

Sacred Scriptures
Koran

Problem No. 22

KEY TO HOLY QURAN

Index – cum – concordance for the Holy Quran

by

Altaf Husain Kherie

THE HOLY QURAN SOCIETY OF PAKISTAN

Karachi

1974

- Class No. 297.203
- Book No. L 4
- Accession No. 136557
- Pages : i-v and 6 to 1084
- Size : 20½ centimeter
- The book is in English language

297.203 L 4	Koran. *English.*
136557	Key to holy Quran : index-cum-concordance for the holy Quran / by Altaf Ahmad Kherie. – Karachi : The Holy Quran Society of Pakistan, 1974. 1084 p. ; 21 cm. 1. Koran – concordance. 2. Kherie, Altaf Ahmad. 3. Title.

Note : In accordance with AACR rule No. 25.17, main entry is to be made under Koran mentioning the name of language of the document and make reference entries from variants.

297. 203 L 4	KORAN-CONCORDANCE Koran. *English.*
	Key to holy Quran : index-cum-concordance for the holy Quran / by Altaf Ahmad Kherie. – Karachi : The Holy Quran Society of Pakistan, 1974. 1084 p. ; 21 cm.

297.203 L 4	Kherie, Altaf Ahmad Koran. *English.*
	Key to holy Quran : index-cum-concordance for the holy Quran / by Altaf Ahmad Kherie. – Karachi : The Holy Quran Society of Pakistan, 1974. 1084 p. ; 21 cm.

297.203 L 4	Koran. *English.*	Key to holy Quran.
	Key to holy Quran : index-cum-concordance for the holy Quran / by Altaf Ahmad Kherie. – Karachi : The Holy Quran Society of Pakistan, 1974.	
	1084 p. ; 21 cm.	

Al-Quran

see Koran

Quran

see Koran

Al-Koran

see Koran

Kalam Majeed

see Koran

Sacred Scriptures
Koran

Problem No. 23

EL-KORAN
Or
THE KORAN

Translated from the Arabic

by
J. M. Rodwell

Wyman & Co. Ltd.
London

1876

- Class No. 297.203
- Book No. A76
- Accession No. 123361
- Size : 21 ½ : centimeters
- Pages : i-v and 6-562
- The book is in English language

297.203 A 76	Koran. English.
123361	El-Koran, or, The Koran / translated from the Arabic / by J. M. Rodwell. – London : Wyman, 1876 562 p. ; 22 cm. 1. Islam – Quran 2. Rodwell, J.M., tr. 3. Title 4. Title : The Koran

When the book has an alternate title, put a comma (,) after the title proper (Main title), then write 'or' and again put a comma, then alternate title, as per illustration given in AACR – II, under rule No. 2.1C.

297.203 A 76	ISLAM – QURAN Koran. English.
	El-Koran, or, The Koran / translated from the Arabic / by J. M. Rodwell. – London : Wyman, 1876 562 p. ; 22 cm.

Note: Reference entries to Koran are to be constructed

297.203	Rodwell, J.M., tr.
A 76	Koran. English.
	El-Koran, or, The Koran / translated from the Arabic / by J. M. Rodwell. – London : Wyman, 1876.
	562 p. ; 22 cm.

297.203	El-Koran.
A 76	Koran. English.
	El-Koran, or, The Koran / translated from the Arabic J. / by M. Rodwell. – London : Wyman, 1876.
	562 p. ; 22 cm.

297.203	The Koran.
A 76	Koran. English.
	El-Koran, or, The Koran / translated from the Arabic / by J. M. Rodwell. – London : Wyman, 1876.
	562 p. ; 22 cm.

Sacred Scriptures Problem No. 24
Tripataka

DHAMMAPADA
WITH
ACCOMPANYING NARRATIVES

Translated from
Chinese

by
Samuel Beat

Second Edition

Shashi Sengupta & Company Ltd.,
CALCUTTA

1956

- Class No. 294.382
- Book No. J 6
- Pages : i-ix and 1-152
- Accession No. 140232
- Size : 25.5 centimeters

294.382
J 6

Tripataka. Suttapitaka. Khuddakanikaya. Dhammapada.

Dhammapada with accompanying narratives / translated from Chinese by Samuel Beat. – 2nd ed. – Calcutta : Shashi Sengupta, 1956.

140232

ix, 152 p. ; 23 cm.

1. Buddhist scriptures 2. Beat, Samuel, tr. 3. Title

294.382
J 6

BUDDHIST SCRIPTURES

Tripataka. Suttapitaka. Khuddakanikaya. Dhammapada.

Dhammapada with accompanying narratives / translated from Chinese by Samuel Beat. – 2nd ed. – Calcutta : Shashi Sengupta, 1956.

ix, 152 p. ; 23 cm.

294.382
J 6

Beat, Samuel, tr.

Tripataka. Suttapitaka. Khuddakanikaya. Dhammapada.

Dhammapada with accompanying narratives / translated from Chinese by Samuel Beat. – 2nd ed. – Calcutta : Shashi Sengupta, 1956.

ix, 152 p. ; 23 cm.

294.382
J 6

Dhammapada with accompanying narratives

Tripataka. Suttapitaka. Khuddakanikaya. Dhammapada.

Dhammapada with accompanying narratives / translated from Chinese by Samuel Beat. – 2nd ed. – Calcutta : Shashi Sengupta, 1956.

ix, 152 p. ; 23 cm.

Sacred Scriptures
Vedas

Problem No. 25

ATHUR VEDAS
with
Extracts from
Religious Books
and
Explanation

Translated from Sanskrit

by
Dr. Kailash Nath Shastri

Galaxy Book Store
MADRAS

1945

- Class No. 294.15
- Book No. H5
- Pages : i-vi and 1-790
- Size : 23½ centimeters
- Accession No. 114321
- The book is in English language

294.15 H 5	Vedas. *Athurveda. English.*
	Athur Vedas with extracts from religious books and explanation / translated from Sanskrit by Kailash Nath Shastri. – Madras : Galaxy Book Store, 1945. vi, 790 p.; 24 cm.
114321	1. Hindu religion scripture 2. Shastri, Kailash Nath, *tr.* 3. Title.

294.15 H 5	HINDU RELIGION SCRIPTURE Vedas. *Athurveda. English*
	Athur Vedas with extracts from religious books and explanation / translated from Sanskrit by Kailash Nath Shastri. – Madras : Galaxy Book Store, 1945. vi, 790 p. ; 24 cm.

294.15 H 5	Athur Vedas with extracts from religious ... Vedas. *Athurveda. English.*
	Athur Vedas with extracts from religious books and explanation / translated from Sanskrit by Kailash Nath Shastri. – Madras : Galaxy Book Store, 1945. vi, 790 p. ; 24 cm.

294.15 H 5	Shastri, Kailash Nath, *tr.* Vedas. *Athurveda. English.*
	Athur Vedas with extracts from religious books and explanation / translated from Sanskrit by Kailash Nath Shastri. – Madras : Galaxy Book Store, 1945. vi, 790 p. ; 24 cm.

Anonymous Classics
Arabian Nights

Problem No. 26

MORE STORIES
from
THE ARABIAN NIGHTS

Translated by
Richard Burton

Edited by
Julian Franklyn

HAMILTON & COMPANY Ltd.
London

1981

- Class No. 0111,28,3x
- Book No. M 1
- Pages : i-v and 1-219
- Size : 23½ centimeters
- Accession No. 135432

0111,28,3x M 1	Arabian Nights
135432	More stories from the Arabian nights / edited by Julian Franklyn; translated by Richard Burton, illustrated by McDonald Sinclair. – London : Hamilton, 1981. vi, 219 p. : ill. ; 22 cm. 1. English literature – Stories. 2. Franklyn, Julian, *ed.* 3. Burton, Richard, *tr.* 4. Sinclair, McDonald, *ill.* 5. Title

0111,28, 3x M 1	ENGLISH LITERATURE – STORIES Arabian Nights
	More stories from the Arabian nights / edited by Julian Franklyn; translated by Richard Burton, illustrated by McDonald Sinclair. – London : Hamilton, 1981. vi, 219 p. : ill. ; 22 cm.

0111,28, 3x M 1	Franklyn, Julian, *ed.* Arabian Nights
	More stories from the Arabian nights / edited by Julian Franklyn; translated by Richard Burton, illustrated by McDonald Sinclair. – London : Hamilton, 1981. vi. 219 p. : ill. ; 22 cm.

0111,28, 3x M 1	Arabian Nights	Burton, Richard, *tr.*
		More stories from the Arabian nights / edited by Julian Franklyn; translated by Richard Burton, illustrated by McDonald Sinclair. – London : Hamilton, 1981. vi, 219 p. : ill. ; 22 cm.

0111,28, 3x M 1	Arabian Nights	Sinclair, McDonald, *ill.*
		More stories from the Arabian nights / edited by Julian Franklyn; translated by Richard Burton, illustrated by McDonald Sinclair. – London : Hamilton, 1981. vi, 219 p. : ill. ; 22 cm.

0111,28, 3x M 1	Arabian Nights	More stories from the Arabian nights
		More stories from the Arabian nights / edited by Julian Franklyn; translated by Richard Burton, illustrated by McDonald Sinclair. – London : Hamilton, 1981. vi. 219 p. : ill. ; 22 cm.

Anonymous Classics Problem No. 27

RIP VAN WINKLE

by
Lanncelot Wagstaffe

Drawings by
Arthur Rackham

LIPPINCOT Inc.
Philadelphia

1967

- Class No. 813.2
- Book No. K 7
- Accession No. 135432
- Size : 23½ centimeters
- Pages : i-v and 1-219
- Reference sources revealed that the name of Lancelot Wagstaffe is identified as Washington Irving

813.2 K 7	Irving, Washington
135432	Rip Van Winkle / by Lanncelot Wagestaffe ; drawings by Arthur Rackham. – Philadelphia : Lippincott, 1967. v, 219, 64 p. : ill. ; 24 cm. 1. American – fiction 2. Rackham, Arthur, *ill.* 3. Title

813.2 K 7	AMERICAN – FICTION Irving, Washington
	Rip Van Winkle / by Lanncelot Wagestaffe ; drawings by Arthur Rackham. – Philadelphia : Lippincott, 1967. v, 219 : ill. ; 24 cm.

813.2 K 7	Rackham, Arthur, *ill.* Irving, Washington
	Rip Van Winkle / by Lanncelot Wagestaffe ; drawings by Arthur Rackham. – Philadelphia : Lippincott, 1967. v, 219 p. : ill. ; 24 cm.

813.2 Rip Van Winkle
K 7 Irving, Washington

Rip Van Winkle / by Lanncelot Wagestaffe ; drawings by Arthur Rackham. – Philadelphia : Lippincott, 1967.

v, 219 p. : ill. ; 24 cm.

Name Reference Entry

Wagestaffe, Lanncelot

see Irving, Washington

Pseudonyms
Single Pseudonym

Problem No. 28

FOLLOWING
THE
EQUATOR

A Journey Around the World

by
Mark Twain

George Allen & Unwin Co. Ltd.
London .. Paris .. New York

1925

- Class No. 0111,3M35
- Book No. F 5
- Pages : i-v and 6-223 centimeter
- The real name of the author is : Samuel Langhorne Clemens
- Accession No. 125315
- Size : 19 ¼ centimeters

0111,3M35 F 5	Twain, Mark	
	Following the equator : a journey around the world / by Mark Twain. – London ; New York : George Allen & Unwin, 1925. 223 p. ; 20 cm.	
125315	1. English – fiction. 2. Title	

0111,3M35 F 5	ENGLISH – FICTION Twain, Mark	
	Following the equator : a journey around the world / by Mark Twain. – London ; New York : George Allen & Unwin, 1925. 223 p. ; 20 cm.	

0111,3M35 F 5	Following the equator Twain, Mark	
	Following the equator : a journey around the world / by Mark Twain. – London ; New York : George Allen & Unwin, 1925. 223 p. ; 20 cm.	

Reference Entry from Real Name

	Clemens, Samuel Langhorne	
	see Twain, Mark	

Pseudonyms – Several Pseudonyms Problem No. 29
Dominant Name

REBEL ON THE RANGE

by
Ranger Lee

The Greystone Press, Inc.
New York

1925

- Class No. 823
- Book No. F 5
- Accession No. 231221
- Pages : i-v and 6-292 centimeter
- The real name of the author is Charles Horace Snow
- The author also wrote under his real name and under other pseudonyms:
  - — Charles Ballew
  - — Gary Marshal
  - — Chester Will
  - — Russ Hardy

  But he is
  - — Famous as Ranger Lee

823		
F 5	Lee, Ranger	
		Rebel on the range / by Ranger Lee. – New York : The Greystone Press, 1925.
		292 p. ; 22 cm.
231221		1. English – fiction. 2. Title

823		ENGLISH – FICTION
F 5	Lee, Ranger	
		Rebel on the range / by Ranger Lee. – New York : The Greystone Press, 1925.
		292 p. ; 22 cm.

823		Rebel on the range.
F 5	Lee, Ranger	
		Rebel on the range / by Ranger Lee. – New York : The Greystone Press, 1925.
		292 p. ; 22 cm.

Reference Entry from Real Name

	Snow, Charles Hornace	
		see Lee, Ranger

Note : This author has adopted several pseudonyms but he is pre-dominantly famous by pseudonym 'Ranger Lee'. Main entry has been made under 'Lee, Ranger' and

Reference entries from Real name and other pseudonyms have been made to 'Lee, Ranger'.

Reference Entries from Other Pseudonyms

	Ballew, Charles	
		see Lee, Ranger

	Hardey, Russ	
		see Lee, Ranger

	Marshal, Gary	
		see Lee, Ranger

	Will, Chester	
		see Lee, Ranger

Several Pseudonyms
No Dominant Name

Problem No. 30

THE EDGE OF TERROR

by

Michael Halliday

J.J. Lippincott and Company Inc.

PHILADELPHIA

1948

- Class No. 823
- Book No. H 8
- Pages : i-v & 6-321 centimeter
- Accession No. 192341
- Size : 22 centimeter
- The real name of the author is John Creasey, who has also written his under real name.
- The author also used the other pseudonyms given below in other books but is not known predominantly in any one of them:
  - — Anthony Morton
  - — Gordon Ashe
  - — J.J. Marric
  - — Jeremy York

823 H 8	Halliday, Michael
192341	The edge of terror / by Michael Halliday. – Philadelphia : J.J. Lippincott, 1948. 321 p. ; 22 cm. 1. English – fiction. 2. Title

823 H 8	ENGLISH FICTION Halliday, Michael
	The edge of terror / by Michael Halliday. – Philadelphia : J.J. Lippincott, 1948. 321 p. ; 22 cm.

823 H 8	The Edge of terror Halliday, Michael
	The edge of terror / Michael Halliday. – Philadelphia : J.J. Lippincott 1948. 321 p. ; 22 cm.

Reference Entry from Real Name

	Creasy, John
	For works of this author written under pseudonyms, see Ashe, Gordon Marric, J.J. Morton, Anthony York, Jeremy

Reference Entries from Other Pseudonyms

	Ashe, Gordon
	For works of this author written under his real name, see Creasey, John For works written under his other pseudonyms, see Marric, J.J. Morton, Anthony York, Jeremy

	Marric, J.J.
	For works of this author written under his real name, see Creasey, John For works written under his other pseudonyms, see Ashe, Gordon Morton, Anthony York, Jeremy

Morton, Anthony

For works of this author written under his real name, see

Creasey, John

For works written under his other pseudonyms, see

Ashe, Gordon

Marric, J.J.

York, Jeremy

York, Jeremy

For works of this author written under his real name, see

Creasey, John

For works written under his other pseudonyms, see

Ashe, Gordon

Marric, J.J.

Morton, Anthony

Shared / Joint Pseudonym Problem No. 31

HAUNTED HOUSE

by
Frederick Evan

Illustrated
by
Richard Burton

Sage Publication Ltd.
London

1969

- Class No. 0111,3M92,7
- Size : 22½ x 10¼ centimeter
- Pages : i-v & 1-290
- The real names of the author as found in Reference Sources are Robert Smith and Manning Bonn. All works of the authors appeared in their Joint pseudonym.
- Accession No. 154321
- Book No. K9

0111,3M92,7		
K 9	Evan	Frederick
		Haunted house / by Frederick Evan; illustrated by Richard Burton. – London : Sage Publications, 1969.
		v, 290 p. : ill. ; 23 x 11 cm.
154321		1. English – fiction. 2. Burton, Richard, *ill.* 3. Title .

0111,3M92,7		ENGLISH – FICTION
K 9	Evan	Frederick
		Haunted house / by Frederick Evan; illustrated by Richard Burton. – London : Sage Publications, 1969.
		v, 290 p. : ill. ; 23 x 11 cm.

0111,3M92,7		Haunted house
K 9	Evan	Frederick
		Haunted house / by Frederick Evan; illustrated by Richard Burton. – London : Sage Publications, 1969.
		v, 290 p. : ill. ; 23 x 11 cm.

0111,3M92,7 K 9	Evan, Frederick	Burton, Richard, *ill.*
	Haunted house / by Frederick Evan; illustrated by Richard Burton. – London : Sage Publications, 1969. v, 290 p. : ill. ; 23 x 11 cm.	

Note : Shared or Joint Pseudonym: Two explanatory reference entries are to be made; one from the real name of the first author to Joint Pseudonym and the other from the real name of the second author, as illustrated below:

	Smith, Robert	
	For works of this author written in collaboration with Manning Bonn, see Evan, Frederick	

	Bonn, Manning	
	For works of this author written in collaboration with Robert Smith, see Evan, Frederick	

Collection
With Collective Title

Problem No. 32

FACETS OF NEHRU

by
S. Radhakrishnan
Humayun Kabir
V.K.R.V. Rao

Edited by
B.K. Ahluwalia

S.E.S. & Co.
Fountain
Delhi

1969

- Class No. V44&y7M89
- Book No. K9
- Pages : i-v & 1-97
- Accession No. 14321
- Chapter - 1 : Jawaharlal Nehru by S. Radhakrishnan
  — Class No. V44&y7M89
- Chapter - 2 : Nehru as a man of letters by Humayun Kabir
  — Class No. Q&aV44y7M89
- Chapter - 3 : Nehru and India's cultural renaissance By V.K.R.V. Rao
  — Class No. Y744:18&V44y7M89
- Size : 19 centimeters

V44&y7M89 K 9	Facets of Nehru / edited by B.K. Ahluwalia. – Delhi	
14321	: S.E.S., 1969. v, 97 p. ; 19 cm. Contents : Chap. 1. Jawaharlal Nehru / by S. Radhakrishnan – Chap. 2 Nehru as a man of letters / by Humayun Kabir – Chap. 3. Nehru and India's cultural renaissance / by V.K.R.V. Rao. 1. India – cultural heritage. 2. Ahluwalia, B.K., *ed.* 3. Radhakrishnan, S. 4. Humayun Kabir 5. Rao, V.K.R.V.	

V44&y7M89 K 9	INDIA – CULTURAL HERITAGE Facets of Nehru / edited by B.K. Ahluwalia. – Delhi	
	: S.E.S., 1969. v, 97 p. ; 19 cm. Contents : Chap. 1. Jawaharlal Nehru / by S. Radhakrishnan – Chap. 2 Nehru as a man of letters / by Humayun Kabir – Chap. 3. Nehru and India's cultural renaissance / by V.K.R.V. Rao.	

V44&y7M89 K 9	Ahluwalia, B.K., ed. Facets of Nehru / edited by B.K. Ahluwalia. – Delhi	
	: S.E.S., 1969. v, 97 p. ; 19 cm. Contents : Chap. 1. Jawaharlal Nehru / by S. Radhakrishnan – Chap. 2 Nehru as a man of letters / by Humayun Kabir – Chap. 3. Nehru and India's cultural renaissance / by V.K.R.V. Rao.	

Note : For all the Contributors of the book, author analytical entries, in accordance with AACR-II rule No. 13.5 (*In* – Analytical) are to be prepared with word 'In' to be italicized or underlined. Illustration is given below:

V44&y7 M89 K 9	Radhakrishnan, S.
	Jawaharlal Nehru / by S. Radhakrishnan. Chap. 1. *In* Facets of Nehru / edited by B.K. Ahluwalia. – Delhi : S.E.S., 1969.

V44&y7M89 K 9	Humayun Kabir
	Nehru as a man of letters / by Humayun Kabir. Chap. 2. *In* Facets of Nehru / edited by B.K. Ahluwalia. – Delhi : S.E.S., 1969

V44&y7M89 K 9	Rao, V.K.R.V.
	Nehru and India's cultural renaissance / by V.K.R.V. Rao. Chap. 3. *In* Facets of Nehru / edited by B.K. Ahluwalia. – Delhi : S.E.S., 1969

Name Reference Entry

	Kabir, Humayun
	see Humayun Kabir

Collection
With Collective Title

Problem No. 33

NEW DIMENSION OF PHILOSOPHY & ETHICS

by
Dr. Hari Ram Gupta
Dr. Ram Nath Jha
Dr. Om Prakash Rastogi
and
Dr. Suraj Bhan Suri

(Second Edition)

Galaxy Book House Limited
Jaipur

1976

- Class No. R
- Book No. L 6
- Pages : i-v and 1-145
- Accession No. 115134
- Size : 22.25 centimeters

Contents

... Chapter - 1 : Logic of Scientific Method by Dr. Hari Ram Gupta and Dr. Ram Nath Jha — Class No. R17

... Chapter - 2 : Social Etiquette by Dr. Om Prakash Rastogi — Class No. R434

... Chapter - 3 : Metaphysical Study of Materialism by Dr. Suraj Bhan Suri — Class No. R33

* Galaxy Series of Social Etics and Logic No. XXI

R L 6		New dimension of philosophy & ethic. 2nd ed.–Jaipur:
115134		Galaxy Book House, 1976. v, 145 p. ; 23 cm. – (Galaxy series of social ethics and logic ; 21) Contents : Ch. 1. Logic of scientific method / by Hari Ram Gupta and Ram Nath Jha – Ch. 2. Social etiquette / by Om Prakash Rastogi – Ch. 3. Metaphysical study of materialism / by Suraj Bhan Suri. 1. Philosophy 2. Ethics 3. Series 4. Gupta, Hari Ram 5. Jha, Ram Nath 6. Rastogi, Om Prakash 7. Suri, Suraj Bhan

R L 6		PHILOSOPHY New dimension of philosophy & ethic. – 2nd ed. –
		Jaipur : Galaxy Book House, 1976. v, 145 p. ; 23 cm. – (Galaxy series of social ethics and logic ; 21) Contents : Ch. 1. Logic of scientific method / by Hari Ram Gupta and Ram Nath Jha – Ch. 2. Social etiquette / by Om Prakash Rastogi – Ch. 3. Metaphysical study of materialism / by Suraj Bhan Suri.

R
L 6

ETHICS
New dimension of Philosophy & ethic – 2nd ed. –
Jaipur : Galaxy Book House, 1976.
v, 145 p. ; 23 cm. – (Galaxy series of social ethics and logic ; 21)
Contents : Ch. 1. Logic of scientific method / by Hari Ram Gupta and Ram Nath Jha – Ch. 2. Social etiquette / by Om Prakash Rastogi – Ch. 3 . Metaphysical study of materialism / by Suray Bhan Suri.

O

R
L 6

Galaxy series of social of social science and logic; 21
New dimension of Philosophy & ethic – 2nd ed. –
Jaipur : Galaxy Book House, 1976.
v, 145 p. ; 23 cm. – (Galaxy series of social ethics and logic ; 2)
Contents : Ch. 1. Logic of scientific method / by Hari Ram Gupta and Ram Nath Jha – Ch. 2. Social etiquette / by Om Prakash Rastogi – Ch. 3 . Metaphysical study of materialism / by Suraj Bhan Suri.

O

Author Analytical for Contributor

R L 6	Gupta, Hari Ram	
	Logic of scientific method / by Hari Ram Gupta and Ram Nath Jha. Ch. 1. *In* New dimension of philosophy & ethics. – 2nd ed. – Jaipur : Galaxy Book House, 1976.	

Author Analytical for Joint Contributor

R L 6	Jha, Ram Nath Gupta, Hari Ram	
	Logic of scientific method / by Hari Ram Gupta and Ram Nath Jha. Ch. 1. *In* New dimension of philosophy & ethics. – 2nd ed. – Jaipur : Galaxy Book House, 1976.	

Author Analytical for Contributor 2

R L 6	Rastogi, Om Prakash	
	Social etiquette / by Om Prakash Rastogi. Ch. 2. *In* New dimension of philosophy & ethics. – 2nd ed. – Jaipur : Galaxy Book House, 1976.	

Author Analytical for Contributor - 3

R L 6	Suri, Suraj Bhan	
	Metaphysical study of materialism / by Suraj Bhan Suri. Ch. 3. *In* New dimension of philosophy & ethics. – 2nd ed. – Jaipur : Galaxy Book House, 1976.	

Collection
With Collective Title

Problem No. 34

Modern Series of Population & Demography No. IX

GEOGRAPHY AND A CROWDING WORLD

A Study on Population
and
Social Resources

by
Dr. Yogesh Charan
Dr. Bhupal Rai Johri
and
Dr. P. Sen Gupta

Oriental Book House Ltd., Jodhpur

1970

- Class No. Y : 52
- Book No. L
- Pages : i-v and 1-312
- Accession No. 136215
- Size : 22½ centimeters

Contents:

- Part - I : Increasing Agricultural Output and Population by Dr. Yogesh Charan Class No. Y:52:(XB(J) : 2
- Part - II : Demographic Resources and Mountain Life by Dr. Bhupal Rai Johri Class No. Y:5
- Part - III : Population and Resources Development in India by Dr. P Sen Gupta Class No. Y:5(X:27).44

Y : 52 L	Geography and a crowding world : a study on population and social resources. – Jodhpur : Oriental Book House, 1970.
	v, 312 p. ; 23 cm. – (Modern series of population & demography ; 9).
136215	Contents : pt. 1. Increasing agricultural output and population / by Yogesh Charan – pt. 2. Demographic resources and mountain life / by Bhupal Rai Johri – pt. 3. Population and resources development / by P. Sen Gupta.
	1. Demography 2. Series 3. Yogesh Charan 4. Johri, Bhupal Rai 5. Sen Gupta, P.

Y:52 L	DEMOGRAPHY Geography and a crowding world : a study on population and social resources. – Jodhpur : Oriental Book House, 1970.
	v, 312 p. ; 23 cm. – (Modern series of population & demography ; 9).
	Contents : pt. 1. Increasing agricultural output and population / by Yogesh Charan – pt. 2. Demographic resources and mountain life / by Bhupal Rai Johri – pt. 3. Population and resources development / by P. Sen Gupta.

Y:52 Modern series of population & demography; 9
L Geography and a crowding world : a study on population and social resources. – Jodhpur : Oriental Book House, 1970.

v, 312 p. ; 23 cm. – (Modern series of population & demography ; 9).

Contents : pt. 1. Increasing agricultural output and population / by Yogesh Charan – pt. 2. Demographic resources and mountain life / by Bhupal Rai Johri – pt. 3. Population and resources development / by P. Sen Gupta.

Author Analytical for Contributor 1

Y:52
L Yogesh Charan

Increasing agricultural output and population / by Yogesh Charan. pt.1

In Geography and a crowding world : a study on population and social resources. – Jaipur : Oriental Book House, 1970.

Author Analytical for Contributor – 2

Y:52
L Johri, Bhupal Rai

Demographic resources and mountain life / by Bhupal Rai Johri. pt. 2.

In Geography and a crowding world : a study on population and social resources. – Jaipur : Oriental Book House, 1970.

Author Analytical for Contributor 3

Y:52 L	Sen Gupta, P.	
	Population and resources development / by P. Sen Gupta. pt. 3. *In* Geography and a crowding world : a study on population and social resources. – Jaipur : Oriental Book House, 1970.	

Name Reference Entry

	Gupta, P. Sen	
		see Sen Gupta, P.

Collection Problem No. 35
Without Collective Title

NUCLEAR ENERGY AND MECHANICS

by

Prof. Edward I. Nixon

and

Dr. Frances J. Rew

FUNDAMENTALS OF THEORETICAL MECHANICS

by

Dr. Charles B. Lancaster

STRUCTURAL GENERATION OF NUCLEAR ENERGY

by

Dr. Braine F. Hudson

ELECTRIC GENERATION & NUCLEAR MECHANICS

by

Dr. Henry L. Green

A.R. SIMLEY PRINTS Ltd.,
London

- Class No. D71.1
- Book No. M 2
- Pages Work - I : Pages i-v and 6-97 : Class No. D71:1
- Pages Work - II : Pages 98-150 : Class No. B7: 1
- Pages Work - III : Pages 152-210 : Class No. D71:11
- Pages Work - IV : Pages 212-350 : Class No. D66171:1
- Accession No. 112560
- Size : 23¼ centimeters
- Copyrights : May, 1982
- The book contains charts, diagrams, pictures, tables etc.

Note : All the four works were published together in one volume by special arrangements and mutual consent with respective Publishers and Copyright-holders and a fresh Copyright was obtained in May, 1982.

D71:1 M 2	Nixon, Edward I.
	Nuclear energy and mechanics / by Edward I. Nixon and Francis J. Rew. Fundamentals of theoretical mechanics / by Charles B. Lancaster. Structural generation of nuclear energy / by Braine F. Hudson. Electronic generation & nuclear mechanics / by Henry L. Green. – London : A.R. Simley Prints, ©1982. 97, 98-150, 152-210, 212-350 p.: ill. ; 24 cm. 1. Nuclear energy 2. Rew, Francis J. 3. Title 4. Mechanics 5. Lancaster, Charles B. Funda... 6. Hudson, Braine F. Struc. ... 7. Electric generation 8. Green, Henry L. Electric ...

D71:1 M 2	NUCLEAR ENERGY Nixon, Edward I.
	Nuclear energy and mechanics / by Edward I. Nixon and Francis J. Rew. Fundamentals of theoretical mechanics / by Charles B. Lancaster. Structural generation of nuclear energy / by Braine F. Hudson. Electronic generation & nuclear mechanics / by Henry L. Green. – London : A.R. Simley Prints, ©1982. 97, 98-150, 152-210, 212-350 p. : ill. ; 24 cm.

D71:1 Rew, Francis J.
M 2 Nixon, Edward I.

Nuclear energy and mechanics / by Edward I. Nixon and Francis J. Rew. Fundamentals of theoretical mechanics / by Charles B. Lancaster. Structural generation of nuclear energy / by Braine F. Hudson. Electronic generation & nuclear mechanics / by Henry L. Green. – London : A.R. Simley Prints, c1982.

97, 98-150, 152-210, 212-350 p. : ill. ; 24 cm.

D71:1 Nuclear energy and mechanics
M 2 Nixon, Edward I.

Nuclear energy and mechanics / by Edward I. Nixon and Francis J. Rew. Fundamentals of theoretical mechanics / by Charles B. Lancaster. Structural generation of nuclear energy / by Braine F. Hudson. Electronic generation & nuclear mechanics / by Henry L. Green. – London : A.R. Simley Prints, c1982.

97, 98-150, 152-210, 212-350 p. : ill. ; 24 cm.

Subject Analytical for Charles B. Lancaster

D71:1 M 2	MECHANICS Lancaster, Charles B. Nixon, Edward I.
	Nuclear energy and mechanics / by Edward I. Nixon and Francis J. Rew. Fundamentals of theoretical mechanics / by Charles B. Lancaster. Structural generation of nuclear energy / by Braine F. Hudson. Electronic generation & nuclear mechanics / by Henry L. Green. – London : A.R. Simley Prints, ᶜ1982. 97, 98-150, 152-210, 212-350 p. : ill. ; 24 cm.

Name-Title Analytical Entry

D71:1 M 2	Lancaster, Charles B. Fundamentals of theoretical of theoretical Nixon, Edward I.
	Nuclear energy and mechanics / by Edward I. Nixon and Francis J. Rew. Fundamentals of theoretical mechanics / by Charles B. Lancaster. Structural generation of nuclear energy / by Braine F. Hudson. Electronic generation & nuclear mechanics / by Henry L. Green. – London : A.R. Simley Prints, ᶜ1982. 97, 98-150, 152-210, 212-350 p. : ill. ; 24 cm.

Name – Title Analytical Entry

D71:1 M 2	Nixon, Edward I.	Hudson, Braine F. Structural generation of nuclear energy
		Nuclear energy and mechanics / by Edward I. Nixon and Francis J. Rew. Fundamentals of theoretical mechanics / by Charles B. Lancaster. Structural generation of nuclear energy / by Braine F. Hudson. Electronic generation & nuclear mechanics / by Henry L. Green. – London : A.R. Simley Prints, ©1982. 97, 98-150, 152-210, 212-350 p. : ill. ; 24 cm. ○

Subject Analytical for Henry L. Green

D71:1 M 2	Nixon, Edward I.	ELECTRIC GENERATION Green, Henry L.
		Nuclear energy and mechanics / by Edward I. Nixon and Francis J. Rew. Fundamentals of theoretical mechanics / by Charles B. Lancaster. Structural generation of nuclear energy / by Braine F. Hudson. Electronic generation & nuclear mechanics / by Henry L. Green. – London : A.R. Simley Prints, ©1982. 97, 98-150, 152-210, 212-350 p. : ill. ; 24 cm. ○

Name – Title Analytical Entry

D71:1 M 2	Green, Henry L. Electric generation of nuclear Nixon, Edward I.
	Nuclear energy and mechanics / by Edward I. Nixon and Francis J. Rew. Fundamentals of theoretical mechanics / by Charles B. Lancaster. Structural generation of nuclear energy / by Braine F. Hudson. Electronic generation & nuclear mechanics / by Henry L. Green. – London : A.R. Simley Prints, ©1982. 97, 98-150, 152-210, 212-350 p. : ill. ; 24 cm.

Collection
Without Collective Title
Published Together

Problem No. 36

THE POETRY OF EARTH

An Introduction to Biogeography

by

Dr. James M. Fisher
Dr. Gordon warwick

UNDER WILDERNESS SKIES

by

Prof. Maurice Watchman
in collaboration with
Dr. Weldon P. Smith

GEORGE PROFFER & CO. Ltd.
London, W.C. 1

First work

- Class No. 574.909
- Book No. N 5
- Accession No. 13221
- Size : 23½ x 5½ centimeters
- Pages : i-x and 1-119

Second work

- Class No. 574.9
- Book No. N 5
- Pages : 121 – 423
- Both works contain diagrams, charts, pictures, etc.

Note : First and Second works were published together in one volume with arrangements from the copyright holders under fresh copyrights in May, 1995.

574.909	
N 5	Warwick, Gordon
	The poetry of earth : an introduction to biogeography / by James M. Fisher, Gordon Warwick, under wilderness skies / by Maurice Watchman in collaboration with Weldon P. Smith. – London : George Proffer, ©1995.
	119, 121-423 p. : ill. ; 23 cm.
13221	1. Biogeography 2. Fisher, James M. 3. Title : The Poetry of earth 4. Wilderness 5. Watchman, Maurice 6. Smith, Weldon 7. Title : Under wilderness skies.

574.909	BIOGEOGRAPHY
N 5	Warwick, Gordon
	The poetry of earth : an introduction to biogeography / by James M. Fisher, Gordon Warwick, under wilderness skies / by Maurice Watchman in collaboration with Weldon P. Smith. – London : George Proffer, ©1995.
	119, 121-423 p. : ill. ; 23 cm.

574.909	Fisher, James M.
N 5	Warwick, Gordon
	The poetry of earth : an introduction to biogeography / by James M. Fisher, Gordon Warwick ; under wilderness skies / by Maurice Watchman in collaboration with Weldon P. Smith. – London : George Proffer, ©1995.
	119, 121-423 p. : ill. ; 23 cm.

574.909 The Poetry of earth
N 5 Warwick, Gordon

The poetry of earth : an introduction to biogeography / by James M. Fisher, Gordon Warwick ; under wilderness skies / by Maurice Watchman in collaboration with Weldon P. Smith. – London : George Proffer, c1995.

119, 121-423 p. : ill. ; 23 cm.

574.909 WILDERNESS
N 5 Warwick, Gordon

The poetry of earth : an introduction to biogeography / by James M. Fisher, Gordon Warwick, under wilderness skies / by Maurice Watchman in collaboration with Weldon P. Smith. – London : George Proffer, c1995.

119, 121-423 p. : ill. ; 23 cm.

574.909 Watchman, Maurice
N5 Warwick, Gordon

The poetry of earth : an introduction to biogeography / by James M. Fisher, Gordon Warwick, under wilderness skies / by Maurice Watchman in collaboration with Weldon P. Smith. – London : George Proffer, c1995.

119, 121-423 p. : ill. ; 23 cm.

574.909 N 5	Warwick, Gordon	Smith, Weldon
The poetry of earth : an introduction to biogeography / by James M. Fisher, Gordon Warwick, under wilderness skies / by Maurice Watchman in collaboration with Weldon P. Smith. – London : George Proffer, ©1995. 119, 121-423 p. : ill. ; 23 cm.		

574.909 N 5	Warwick, Gordon	Under wilderness skies
The poetry of earth : an introduction to biogeography / by James M. Fisher, Gordon Warwick, under wilderness skies / by Maurice Watchman in collaboration with Weldon P. Smith. – London : George Proffer, ©1995. 119, 121-423 p. : ill. ; 23 cm.		

Collection Problem No. 37
Without Collective Title Bound together

NORTH AMERICAN INDIAN LANGUAGES
Classification & Maps

by
Prof. George L. Trager
and
Dr. John E. William

University of Buffalo
New York

First work

- Class No. P73
- Book No. J 8
- Pages : i-iv and 1-151
- Accession No. 124316
- Copyrights October 1958
- Size : 22 ¼ centimeters
- International Linguistic Studies No. XII

PHONETICS
Glossary and Tables

by
Prof. John S. Lee
Dr. Charles W. Bone

Second Edition

McMillan & Co. Inc. New York

Second work

- Class No. P: 1k
- Book No. J 8
- Pages : i-xx and 22-43
- Size : 22 ¼ centimeters
- Accession No. 134321

Note : First and Second works have been bound together in the library.

P73
J 8 Trager, George L.

North American Indian languages: classification & maps / by George L. Trager and John E. William. – New York : University of Buffalo, ©1958.

iv, 151 p. : ill. ; 23 cm. – (International linguistic studies ; 2)

124316 With : Phonetics : glossary and tables / by John S. Lee and Charles M. Bone. – 2nd ed. – New York : McMillan, [1958]

1. Linguistics 2. William, John E. 3. Title 4. Series.

LINGUISTICS
P73
J 8 Trager, George L.

North American Indian languages: classification & maps / by George L. Trager and John E. William. – New York : University of Buffalo, ©1958.

iv, 151 p. : ill. ; 23 cm. – (International linguistic studies ; 2)

With : Phonetics : glossary and tables / by John S. Lee and Charles M. Bone. – 2nd ed. – New York : McMillan, [1958]

William, John E.
P73
J 8 Trager, George L.

North American Indian languages: classification & maps / by George L. Trager and John E. William. – New York : University of Buffalo, ©1958.

iv, 151 p. : ill. ; 23 cm. – (International linguistic studies ; 2)

With : Phonetics : glossary and tables / by John S. Lee and Charles M. Bone. – 2nd ed. – New York : McMillan, [1958]

P73
J 8
Trager, George L.

North American Indian languages

North American Indian languages: classification & maps / by George L. Trager and John E. William. – New York : University of Buffalo, c1958.

iv, 151 p. : ill. ; 23 cm. – (International linguistic studies ; 2)

With : Phonetics : glossary and tables / by John S. Lee and Charles M. Bone. – 2nd ed. – New York : McMillan, [1958]

P73
J 8
Trager, George L.

International linguistic studies; 2.

North American Indian languages: classification & maps / by George L. Trager and John E. William. – New York : University of Buffalo, c1958.

iv, 151 p. : ill. ; 23 cm. – (International linguistic studies ; 2)

With : Phonetics : glossary and tables / by John S. Lee and Charles M. Bone. – 2nd ed. – New York : McMillan, [1958]

P73
J 8
Lee, John S.

Phonetics : glossary and tables / by John S. Lee, Charles W. Bone. – 2nd ed. – New York : McMillan, [1958].

134321

143 p. : ill. ; 23 cm.

With : North American Indian languages : classification & maps / by George L. Trager and John E. William. – New York : University of Buffalo, c1958.

1. Phonology 2. Bone, Charles W. 3. Title

Note: In the ME of Second Work, the Class No. and Book No. of the First Work will be given.

P73 J 8	PHONOLOGY Lee, John S.
	Phonetics : glossary and tables / by John S. Lee, Charles W. Bone. – 2nd ed. – New York : McMillan, [1958]. 143 p. : ill. ; 23 cm. With : North American Indian languages : classification & maps / by George L. Trager and John E. William. – New York: University of Buffalo, ©1958.

P73 J 8	Bone, Charles W. Lee, John S.
	Phonetics : glossary and tables / by John S. Lee, Charles W. Bone. – 2nd ed. – New York : McMillan, [1958]. 143 p. : ill. ; 23 cm. With : North American Indian languages : classification & maps / by George L. Trager and John E. William. – New York: University of Buffalo, ©1958.

P73 J 8	Phonetics Lee, John S.
	Phonetics : glossary and tables / John S. Lee, Charles W. Bonde – 2nd ed. – New York : McMillan, [1958]. 143 p. : ill. ; 23 cm. With : North American Indian languages : classification & maps / by George L. Trager and John E. William. – New York : University of Buffalo, ©1958.

Corporate Bodies
Govt. Constitution

Problem No. 38

Government of India

CONSTITUTION
OF
INDIA

As amended upto July
1958

Published by
Manager of Publication Division
Govt. of India
DELHI

1959

- Class No. V44:2
- Book No. J 9
- Pages : i-vi and 1-273
- Size : 24 ½ centimeters
- Accession No. 122134

V44:2 J 9	India	*Constitution.*
122134	1958 1959	Constitution of India, as amended upto July – Delhi : Manager of Publication Division, vi, 273 p. ; 25 cm. 1. Constitution – India. 2. Title

V44:2 J 9	India	CONSTITUTION – INDIA. *Constitution*
	1958 1959	Constitution of India, as amended upto July – Delhi : Manager of Publication Division, vi, 273 p. ; 25 cm.

V44:2 J 9	India	Constitution of India as amended ... *Constitution.*
	1958 1959	Constitution of India, as amended upto July – Delhi : Manager of Publication Division, vi, 273 p. ; 25 cm.

Corporate Bodies
Govt. - Commissions

Problem No. 39

REPORT
of
The Education Commission 1964 - 1966

EDUCATION
&
NATIONAL DEVELOPMENT

Ministry of Education
Government of India

Manager of Publication
Govt. of India
New Delhi

1966

- Class No. T44‘N66‘t
- Book No. K 6
- Chairman of the Commission : Prof. D.S. Kothari
- Pages : i-xiii and 1-692
- Accession No. 113561
- It contains charts, graphs, diagrams, Tables, etc.
- The Commission was set up by Ministry of Education, Govt. of India in 1964; its Report was submitted in 1966

T46 'N66't K 6	India	*Ministry of Education.*
113561		Education & national development : report of Education Commission 1964-66. – New Delhi : Manager of Publication Govt. of India, 1966. xiii, 692 p. : ill. ; 28 cm. Chairman : D.S. Kothari Also known as Kothari Commission report. 1. India – National development. 2. Education – India. 3. Kothari, D.S. 4. Kothari Commission report. 5. Title.

T44'N66't K 6	India	INDIA – NATIONAL DEVELOPMENT. *Ministry of Education.*
		Education & national development : report of Education Commission 1964-1966. – New Delhi : Manager of Publication Govt. of India, 1966. xiii, 692 p. : ill. ; 28 cm. Chairman : D.S. Kothari. Also known as Kothari Commission report.

T44 'N66 't K6	India	Kothari, D.S. *Ministry of Education.*
		Education & national development : report of Education Commission 1964-1966. – New Delhi: Manager of Publication, Govt. of India, 1966. xiii, 692, p. : ill. ; 28 cm. Chairman : D.S. Kothari. Also known as Kothari Commission report.

T44'N66't K6	India.	EDUCATION – INDIA *Ministry of Education.*
		Education & national development : report of Education Commission 1964-1966. – New Delhi: Manager of Publication, Govt. of India, 1966 xiii, 692. p. : ill. ; 28 cm. Chairman : D.S. Kothari. Also known as Kothari Commission report.

T44'N66't K 6	India.	Kothari Commission report. *Ministry of Education.*
		Education & national development : report of Education Commission 1964-1966 – New Delhi: Manager of Publication, Govt. of India, 1966 xiii, 692 p. : ill. ; 28 cm. Chairman : D.S. Kothari. Also known as Kothari Commission report.

T44'N66't K 6	India.	Education & national development. *Ministry of Education.*
		Education & national development : report of Education Commission 1964. – 1966. – New Delhi : Manager of Publication, Govt. of India, 1966. xiii, 692, p. : ill. ; 28 cm. Chairman : D.S. Kothari. Also known as Kothari Commission report.

Corporate Bodies Problem No. 40
Govt.—Committee Report

Government of India
Ministry of Food and Agriculture

REPORT OF THE
EXPERT COMMITTEE ON THE PREVENTION OF SLAUGHTER OF CATTLE IN INDIA

Published by
Manager of Publication
Govt. of India
New Delhi

1955

- Class No. KZ31:527.44'N56't
- Book No. J 5
- Accession No. 113561
- Pages : i-iii and 1-692
- The Committee was set up under the Chairmanship of Dr. P.N. Nanda in 1954 and the Report was submitted in January 1955.

KZ31 : 527. 44N'4't
J 5 India. *Expert Committee on the prevention of slaughter of cattle in India.*

Report of the expert committee on the prevention of slaughter of cattle in India. – New Delhi : Manager of Publication Division, 1955.

113561 iii, 212 p. ; 23 cm. – (Publication / India Ministry of Food and Agriculture ; 407)

Chairman of the Committee : P.N. Nanda.

Also known as Nanda Committee report.

1. Cattle slaughter – India. 2. Nanda, P.N. 3. Title : Nanda Committee report 4. Series

---

KZ31:527. 44 'N5'4't CATTLE SLAUGHTER – INDIA
J 5 India. *Expert Committee on the prevention of slaughter of cattle in India.*

Report of the expert committee on the prevention of slaughter of cattle India. – New Delhi : Manager of Publication, 1955.

iii, 212 p. ; 23 cm. – (Publication / India. Ministry of Food and Agriculture ; 407).

Chairman of the Committee : P.N. Nanda.

Also known as Nanda Committee report.

KZ31:527. 44N'54't Nanda, P.N.
J 5 India. *Expert Committee on the prevention of slaughter of cattle in India.*

Report of the expert committee on the prevention of slaughter of cattle India. – New Delhi : Manager of Publication, 1955.

iii, 212 p. ; 23 cm. – (Publication / India. Ministry of Food and Agriculture ; 407).

Chairman of the Committee : P.N. Nanda.

Also known as Nanda Committee report.

KZ31 : 527.44'N54't Nanda Committee report
J 5 India. *Expert Committee on the prevention of slaughter of cattle in India.*

Report of the expert committee on the prevention of slaughter of cattle India. – New Delhi : Manager of Publication, 1955.

iii, 212 p. ; 23 cm. – (Publication / India. Ministry of Food and Agriculture ; 407).

Chairman of the Committee : P.N. Nanda.

Also known as Nanda Committee report.

KZ31:527.44N'54't		Publication / India. Ministry of Food and ...
J 5	India	*Expert Committee on the prevention of slaughter of cattle in India.*
		Report of the expert committee on the prevention of slaughter of cattle India. – New Delhi : Manager of Publication, 1955.
		iii, 212 p. ; 23 cm. – (Publication / India. Ministry of Food and Agriculture ; 407).
		Chairman of the Committee : P.N. Nanda.
		Also known as Nanda Committee report.

Corporate Bodies
Govt.—Ministry with
Subordinate Organ

Problem No. 41

Ministry of Commerce
Govt. of India
Directorate of Exhibition & Commercial Publicity

India's Trade Agreements With Other Countries in Force on May, 1976

Edited by
Dr. Bhola Kumar Jha
Dy. Secretary

Published by
Manager
Publication Division
New delhi

1977

- Class No. X:54.44
- Book No. L 7
- Pages : i - v and 6-320
- Accession No. 134576
- Size : 23 ½ centimeters
- Contains charts, graphs, diagrams, tables etc.

X:54.44
L 7
India. *Ministry of Commerce, Directorate of Exhibition & Commercial Publicity.*

134576

India's trade agreements with other countries in force in May, 1976 / edited by Bhola Kumar Jha. – New Delhi : Manager Publication Division, 1977.

320 p. : ill. ; 24 cm.

1. Trade agreements – India 2. Jha, Bhola Kumar, *ed.* 3. Trade

---

X:54.44
L 7
TRADE AGREEMENTS – INDIA
India. *Ministry of Commerce, Directorate of Exhibition & Commercial Publicity.*

India's trade agreements with other countries in force on May, 1976 / edited by Bhola Kumar Jha. – New Delhi : Manager Publication Division, 1977.

320 p. : ill. ; 24 cm.

X:54.44
L 7
Jha, Bhola Kumar, ed.
India. *Ministry of Commerce, Directorate of Exhibition & Commercial Publicity.*

India's trade agreements with other countries in force in May, 1976 / edited by Bhola Kumar Jha. – New Delhi : Manager Publication Division, 1977.

320 p. : ill. ; 24 cm.

X:54.44
L 7
India's trade agreements with other ...
India. *Ministry of Commerce, Directorate of Exhibition & Commercial Publicity.*

India's trade agreements with other countries in force in May, 1976 / edited by Bhola Kumar Jha. – New Delhi : Manager Publication Division, 1977.

320 p. : ill. ; 24 cm.

Corporate Bodies
Govt.—Committee Report

Problem No. 42

REPORT OF THE WAGE REVISION COMMITTEE FOR PORT AND DOCK WORKERS FOR MAJOR PORT, 1974

Ministry of Shipping and Transport

Published by
Manager of Publication
Government of India,
New Delhi

1977

- Class No. 331.28
- Accession No. 13098
- Book No. L 7
- Pages : i-vi and 1-354
- Size : 23 ½ centimeters
- Contains charts, graphs, diagrams, tables etc.

331.28 L 7	India.	*Wage Revision Committee for Ports and Dock*
13098		*Workers for Major Ports.* Report of wage revision committee for ports and dock workers for major ports, 1974. – New Delhi : Manager of Publications, 1977. vi, 354 p. : ill.; p. 354; 22 cm. – (Publication / India. Ministry of Shipping & Transport ; 92). Chairman : B.N. Lankar Also known as : Lankar Committee report 1. Wages – Port workers. 2. Lankar, B.N. 3. Title. 4. Title : Lankar Committee Report. 5. Series : Publication (India. Ministry of Shipping & Transport).

331.28 L 7	India.	WAGES – PORT WORKERS *Wage Revision Committee for Ports and Dock*
		Workers for Major Ports. Report of wage revision committee for ports and dock workers for major ports, 1974. – New Delhi : Manager of Publication, 1977. vi, p. 354 p. : ill; 22 cm. – (Publication / India. Ministry of Shipping & Transport ; 92). Chairman : B.N. Lankar. Also known as : Lankar Committee report.

<table>
<tr><td>331.28
L 7</td><td>
India</td><td>Lankar, B.N.
Wage Revision Committee for Ports and Dock</td></tr>
<tr><td></td><td colspan="2">Workers for Major Ports.
Report of wage revision committee for ports and dock workers for major ports, 1974. – New Delhi : Manager of Publications, 1977.
vi, 354 p. : ill. p. 320; 22 cm. – (Publication / India. Ministry of Shipping & Transport ; 92).
Chairman : B.N. Lankar.
Also known as : Lankar Committee report.</td></tr>
</table>

<table>
<tr><td>331.28
L 7</td><td>
India</td><td>Report of the wage revision committee ...
Wage Revision Committee for Ports and Dock</td></tr>
<tr><td></td><td colspan="2">Workers for Major Ports.
Report of wage revision committee for ports and dock workers for major ports, 1974. – New Delhi : Manager of Publications, 1977.
: ill., p.; 354 22 cm. – (Publication / India. Ministry of Shipping & Transport ; 92).
Chairman : B.N. Lankar.
Also known as : Lankar Committee report.</td></tr>
</table>

331.28 Lankar Committee report
L 7 India. *Wage Revision Committee for Ports and Dock Workers for Major Ports.*

Report of wage revision committee for ports and dock workers for major ports, 1974. – New Delhi : Manager of Publications, 1977.

vi : ill. p. 354; 22 cm. – (Publication / India. Ministry of Shipping & Transport ; 92).

Chairman : B.N. Lankar.

Also known as : Lankar Committee report.

331.28 Publication / India. Ministry of shipping... 92
L 7 India. *Wage revision Committee for Ports and Dock Workers for Major Ports.*

Report of wage revision committee for ports and dock workers for major ports, 1974. – New Delhi : Manager of Publications, 1977.

vi, 354 p. : ill.; 22 cm. – (Publication / India. Ministry of Shipping & Transport ; 92).

Chairman : B.N. Lankar

Also known as : Lankar Committee report

Corporate Bodies
Govt.—Ministry

Problem No. 43

MINISTRY OF HOME AFFAIRS
GOVT. OF INDIA

Report
of
The Commissioner of Linguistic
Minorities
1966

Published by the Manager
Publication Division
Govt. of
India
New Delhi

1967

- Class No. 323.106154
- Book No. K 7
- Accession No. 121454
- Size : 22 ½ centimeters
- Pages : i-v and 6-415

323.106154
K 7 India. *Ministry of Home Affairs. Commissioner of Linguistic Minorities.*

Report of the commissioner of linguistic minorities, 1966. – New Delhi : Manager Publication Division, 1967.

121454 415 p. ; 23 cm.

1. Linguistic minorities. 2. Title

323.106154 LINGUISTIC MINORITIES
K 7 India. *Ministry of Home Affairs. Commissioner of Linguistic Minorities.*

Report of the commissioner of linguistic minorities, 1966. – New Delhi : Manager Publication Division, 1967.

415 p. ; 23 cm.

323.106154 Report of the commissioner of linguistic ...
K 7 India. *Ministry of Home Affairs. Commissioner of Linguistic Minorities.*

Report of the commissioner of linguistic minorities, 1966. – New Delhi : Manager Publication Division, 1967.

415 p. ; 23 cm.

Corporate Bodies
Joint Committee Report

Problem No. 44

FINANCING WHEAT PRODUCTION PROGRAMME

Proceedings
of

CCU/CUA Joint Committee on Financing and Operating Centres Conference on Wheat Production

Held at
Ontario University
July 12-15, 1971

Under the Chairmanship
of
Prof. David Smith
and
Prof. Herbert Chapman

Ontario University
Ontario

1972

- Class No. J3:5
- Book No. L 2
- Pages : i-v and 6-345
- Accession No. 121454
- Size : 22 ½ centimeters

J3:5
L2 CCU/CUA Joint Committee on Financing and Operating Centres. *Conference on Wheat Production (1971: Ontario)*

121454 Financing wheat production development programmes: proceedings of CCU/CUA Joint Committee on financing and operating centres conference on wheat production held July 12-15, 1971 at Ontario University. Ontario : Ontario University. 1972.

345 p. ; 27 cm.

Chairman : David Smith and Herbert Chapman.

1. Agriculture-Wheat 2. Smith, David 3. Chapman. Herbert 4. Title .

J 3:5 AGRICULTURE – WHEAT
L2 CCU/CUA Joint Committee on Financing and Operating Centres. *Conference on Wheat Production (1971: Ontario)*

Financing wheat production development programmes: proceedings of CCU/CUA Joint Committee on financing and operating centres conference on wheat production held July 12-15, 1971 at Ontario University. Ontario : Ontario University. 1972.

345 p. ; 27 cm.

Chairman : David Smith and Herbert Chapman.

J 3:5 L2		Smith, David CCU/CUA Joint Committee on Financing and Operating Centres. *Conference on Wheat Production (1971: Ontario)* Financing wheat production development programmes: proceedings of CCU/CUA Joint Committee on financing and operating centres conference on wheat production held July 12-15, 1971 at Ontario University. Ontario : Ontario University. 1972. 345 p. ; 27 cm. Chairman : David Smith and Herbert Chapman.

J 3:5 L2		Chapman, Herbert CCU/CUA Joint Committee on Financing and Operating Centres. *Conference on Wheat Production (1971: Ontario)* Financing wheat production development programmes: proceedings of CCU/CUA Joint Committee on financing and operating centres conference on wheat production held July 12-15, 1971 at Ontario University. Ontario : Ontario University. 1972. 345 p. ; 27 cm. Chairman : David Smith and Herbert Chapman.

J 3:5		Financing wheat production development ...
L2	CCU/CUA Joint Committee on Financing and	
		Operating Centres. *Conference on Wheat Production (1971: Ontario)* Financing wheat production development programmes: proceedings of CCU/CUA Joint Committee on financing and operating centres conference on wheat production held July 12-15, 1971 at Ontario University. Ontario : Ontario University. 1972. 345 p. ; 27 cm. Chairman : David Smith and Herbert Chapman.

Corporate Bodies Problem No. 45
Conference

PROCEEDINGS
OF THE
INTERNATIONAL CONFERENCE ON
MATHEMATICAL LOGIC

held at
Derbyshire

on
15-18 July, 1971

Edited by
Prof. R.E. Gaites
&
Dr. John G. Hayting

North Holland Publishers Ltd.,
AMSTERDAM ... LONDON

1972

- Class No. R14p1, N71
- Book No. L 2
- Size : 21.75 centimeters
- Accession No. 156941
- There are plates, charts, diagrams, tables, etc. in the book.
- Pages : i-ix and 1-515

R 14p1, N71 L 2	International Conference on Mathematical Logic (*1971 : Derbyshire*).
156941	Proceedings of the international conference held at Derbyshire on 15-18 July, 1971 / edited by R.E. Gaites and John G. Hayting. – Amsterdam ; London : North Holland Publishers, 1972. ix, 515 p. : ill. ; 22 cm. 1. Logic – Mathematical, 2. Gaites, R.E., ed. 3. Hayting, John G., *jt.ed.* O

R 14p1, N71 L 2	LOGIC – MATHEMATICAL International Conference on Mathematical Logic (*1971 : Derbyshire*).
	Proceedings of the international conference held at Derbyshire on 15-18 July, 1971 / edited by R.E. Gaites and John G. Hayting. – Amsterdom ; London : North Holland Publishers, 1972. ix, 515 p. : ill. ; 22 cm. O

R 14p1, N71
L 2

Gaites, R.E., *ed.*
International Conference on Mathematical Logic (*1971 : Derbyshire*).
Proceedings of the international conference held at Derbyshire on 15-18 July, 1971 / edited by R.E. Gaites & John G. Hayting. – Amsterdom ; London : North Holland Publishers, 1972.
ix, 515 p. : ill. ; 22 cm.

R 14p1, N71
L 2

Hayting, John G., *jt.ed.*
International Conference on Mathematical Logic (*1971 : Derbyshire*).
Proceedings of the international conference held at Derbyshire on 15-18 July, 1971 / edited by R.E. Gaites & John G. Hayting. – Amsterdom ; London : North Holland Publishers, 1972.
ix, 515 p. : ill. ; 22 cm.

Corporate Bodies
Numbered Conference

Problem No. 46

ORDERING SYSTEMS
FOR
GLOBAL INFORMATION NETWORKS

Proceedings
of the
Third International Study Conference on
Classification Research

Edited by
A. Neelameghan

Published Jointly by
FID/CR and Sarda Ranganathan Endowment for Library Science
DRTC, 31 Church Street,
BANGALORE

- FID Publications No. 553
- Class No. 2:51; fp1, N75
- Book No. L 5
- Size : 24.50 centimeters
- Accession No. 132541
- Pages : i-vii and 1-315

2:51f;1,N75
L 5 International Study Conference on Classification Research (*3rd : 1975 : Bombay*).

Ordering system for global information networks : proceedings / edited by A. Neelameghan. – Bangalore : FID/CR and Sarda Ranganathan Endowment for Library Science, 1975.

132541 vii, 315 p. ; 25 cm. – (FID Publications; 553)

1. Library Classification-Research 2. Neelameghan, A., ed. 3 Title 4. Series

---

2:51f;1,N75 LIBRARY CLASSIFICATION – RESEARCH
L 5 International Study Conference on Classification Research (*3rd : 1975 : Bombay*).

Ordering system for global information networks : proceedings / edited by A. Neelameghan. – Bangalore : FID / CR and Sarda Ranganathan Endowment for Library Science, 1975.

vii, 315 p. ; 25 cm. – (FID Publications; 553)

2:51;p1,N75 L 5	Neelameghan, A., *ed.* International Study Conference on Classification Research (*3rd : 1975 : Bombay*). Ordering system for global information networks : proceedings / edited by A. Neelameghan. – Bangalore : FID/CR and Sarda Ranganathan Endowment for Library Science, 1975. vii, 315 p. ; 25 cm. – (FID Publications; 553)

2:51;p1,N75 L 5	Ordering system for global system networks International Study Conference on Classification Research (*3rd : 1975 : Bombay*). Ordering system for global information networks : proceedings / edited by A. Neelameghan. – Bangalore : FID/CR and Sarda Ranganathan Endowment for Library Science, 1975. vii, 315 p.; 25 cm. – (FID Publications; 553)

2:51;p1,N75 L 5	FID Publications ; 553 International Study Conference on Classification Research (*3rd : 1975 : Bombay*). Ordering system for global information networks : proceedings / edited by A. Neelameghan. – Bangalore : FID / CR and Sarda Ranganathan Endowment for Library Science, 1975. vii, 315 p. : 25 cm. – (FID Publications; 553)

Corporate Bodies
Numbered Conference

Problem No. 47

HIGH TEMPERATURE PHENOMENA AND PRODUCTION

Proceedings
of the
The Third International High Energy
Physics Seminar

held at
PUNE
July 16-18, 1983

Edited by
Dr. Mukesh K. Srivastava
and
Dr. Vijay K. Malhotra

INDIAN INSTITUTE OF THERMODYNAMICS
PUNE

1984

- Class No. C9D8 'p44,N83
- Book No. M 4
- Size : 25.15 x 10.15 centimeters
- Page : i-vi and 1-395
- Thermodynamics Seminar & Symposia Series No. VI
- Contains diagrams, charts, tables, graphs etc.
- Accession No. 132541

C9D8 'p44,N83 M 4	National High Energy Physics Seminar (*3rd : Pune : 1983*).
	High temperature phenomena and production : proceedings of the third National High Energy Physics Seminar held at Pune July 16-18, 1983 / edited by Mukesh K. Srivastava and Vijay K. Malhotra. – Pune : Indian Institute of Thermodynamics, 1984.
132541	vi, 395 p. : ill. ; 26 x 11 cm. – (Thermodynamics seminar & symposia series ; 6).
	1. Thermodynamics 2. Srivastava, Mukesh K., *ed.* 3. Malhotra, Vijay K.; *jt. ed.* 4 Title 5. Series

C9D8 'p44,N83 M 4	THERMODYNAMICS National High Energy Physics Seminar (*3rd : Pune : 1983*).
	High temperature phenomena and production : proceedings of the third National High Energy Physics Seminar held at Pune July 16-18, 1983 / edited by Mukesh K. Srivastava and Vijay K. Malhotra. – Pune : Indian Institute of Thermodynamics, 1984.
	vi, 395 p. : ill. ; 26 x 11 cm. – (Thermodynamics seminar & symposia series ; 6).

C9D'6p44,N83 Srivastava, Mukesh K., *ed.*
M 4 National High Energy Physics Seminar (*3rd : Pune : 1983*).

High temperature phenomena and production : proceedings of the third National High Energy Physics Seminar held at Pune July 16-18, 1983, / edited by Mukesh K. Srivastava and Vijay K. Malhotra. – Pune : Indian Institute of Thermodynamics, 1984.

vi, 395 p. : ill. ; 26 x 11 cm. – (Thermodynamics seminar & symposia series ; 6)

C9D8'p44,N83 Malhotra, Vijay K., *jt. ed.*
M 4 National High Energy Physics Seminar (*3rd : Pune : 1983*).

High temperature phenomena and production : proceedings of the third National High Energy Physics Seminar held at Pune July 16-18, 1983 / edited by Nukesh K. Srivastava and Vijay K. Malhotra. – Pune : Indian Institute of Thermodynamics, 1984.

vi, 395 p. : ill. ; 26 x 11 cm. – (Thermodynamics seminar & symposia series ; 6)

C9D8 'p44,N83 High temperature phenomena and ...
M 4 National High Energy Physics Seminar (*3rd : Pune : 1983*).

High temperature phenomena and production : proceedings of the third National High Energy Physics Seminar held at Pune July 16-18, 1983, edited / by Nukesh K. Srivastava and Vijay K. Malhotra. – Pune : Indian Institute of Thermodynamics, 1984.

vi, 395 p. : ill. ; 26 x 11 cm. – (Thermodynamics seminar & symposia series ; 6)

C9D8 'p44,N83 Thermodynamics seminar & symposia ...
M 4 National High Energy Physics Seminar (*3rd : Pune : 1983*).

High temperature phenomena and production : proceedings of the third National High Energy Physics Seminar held at Pune July 16-18, 1983 / edited by Mukesh K. Srivastava and Vijay K. Malhotra. – Pune : Indian Institute of Thermodynamics, 1984.

vi, 395 p. : ill. ; 26 x 11 cm. – (Thermodynamics seminar & symposia series ; 6)

Corporate Bodies
Institutions

Problem No. 48

NATIONAL COUNCIL OF APPLIED ECONOMIC RESEARCH OF INDIA, DELHI

REVIEW OF INDIAN IRON INDUSTRY

by
Dr. Raj Narain
Chief Analyst
and
Dr. Sita Ram Joshi
Dy. Analyst

Published by
Manager of Publications
NCAERI
Delhi

1966

- Class No. X8(F182). 44
- Book No. K 6
- Page : i-ix and 10-295
- Accession No. 136241
- Size : 22¼ centimeters

X8(F182).44
K 6

National Council of Applied Economic Research of India, *Delhi.*

Review of Indian iron industry / edited by Raj Narain and Sita Ram Joshi. – Delhi: Manager of Publications, NCAERI, 1966.

295 p. ; 23 cm.

136241

1. Iron industry – India. 2. Raj Narain, *ed.* 3. Joshi, Sita Ram, *jt. ed.* 4. Title.

X8(F182).44
K 6

IRON INDUSTRY – INDIA.

National Council of Applied Economic Research of India, *Delhi.*

Review of Indian iron industry / edited by Raj Narain and Sita Ram Joshi. – Delhi: Manager of Publications, NCAERI, 1966.

295 p. ; 23 cm.

X8(F182).44
K 6

Raj Narain, *ed.*

National Council of Applied Economic Research of India, *Delhi.*

Review of Indian iron industry / edited by Raj Narain and Sita Ram Joshi. – Delhi : Manager of Publications, NCAERI, 1966.

295 p. ; 23 cm.

X8(F182).44 K 6		Joshi, Sita Ram, *jt. ed.* National Council of Applied Economic Research of India, *Delhi.* Review of Indian iron industry / edited by Raj Narain and Sita Ram Joshi. – Delhi : Manager of Publications, NCAERI, 1966. 295 p. ; 23 cm.

X8(F182).44 K 6		Review of Indian iron industry. National Council of Applied Economic Research of India, *Delhi.* Review of Indian iron industry / edited by Raj Narain and Sita Ram Joshi. – Delhi: Manager of Publications, NCAERI, 1966. 295 p. ; 23 cm.

Corporate Bodies
Institution

Problem No. 49

FARNHAM AGRICULTURAL BUREAUX COMMONWEALTH INSTITUTE OF BIOLOGICAL CONTROL OTTAWA (ONTARIO)

A CATALOGUE
OF
PARASITES AND PREDATORS OF INSECTS ORIGIN

Prepared under the Supervision of

Dr. D.R. THOMPSON
Director General

COMMONWEALTH INSTITUTE OF BIOLOGICAL CONTROL OTTAWA (Ontario)

- Class No. J:428Fa
- Book No. J 7
- Page : i-ix and 1-314
- Accession No. 171841
- Published in May, 1957
- Size : 25¼ x 10 ¼ centimeters
- Advancement of Biological Science Series No. XXI

J:428Fa J 7	Commonwealth Institute of Biological Control.
	Farnham Agricultural Bureaux, Ottawa.
	A catalogue of parasites and predators of insects origin / prepared under supervision of D.R. Thompson. – Ottawa : Commonwealth Institute of Biological Control, [1957].
171841	ix, 314 p. ; 26 x 11 cm. – (Advancement of biological science series; 21)
	1. Parasite control 2. Thompson, D.R. 3. Title 4. Series

J:428Fa	PARASITE CONTROL
J 7	Commonwealth Institute of Biological Control.
	Farnham Agricultural Bureaux, Ottawa.
	A catalogue of parasites and predators of insects origin / prepared under supervision of D.R. Thompson. – Ottawa : Commonwealth Institute of Biological Control, [1957].
	ix, 314 p. ; 26 x 11 cm. – (Advancement of biological science series; 21)

J:428Fa J 7	Thompson, D.R. Commonwealth Institute of Biological Control. *Farnham Agricultural Bureaux, Ottawa.*
	A catalogue of parasites and predators of insects origin / prepared under supervision of D.R. Thompson. – Ottawa : Commonwealth Institute of Biological Control, [1957]. ix, 314 p. ; 26 x 11 cm. – (Advancement of biological science series; 21)

J:428 Fa J 7	A Catalogue of parasites and predators of ... Commonwealth Institute of Biological Control. *Farnham Agricultural Bureaux, Ottawa.*
	A catalogue of parasites and predators of insects origin / prepared under supervision of D.R. Thompson. – Ottawa : Commonwealth Institute of Biological Control, [1957]. ix, 314 p. ; 26 x 11 cm. – (Advancement of biological science series; 21)

J:428 Fa J 7	Advancement of biological science series; 21 Commonwealth Institute of Biological Control. *Farnham Agricultural Bureaux, Ottawa.*
	A catalogue of parasites and predators of insects origin / prepared under supervision of D.R. Thompson. – Ottawa : Commonwealth Institute of Biological Control, [1957]. ix, 314 p. ; 26 x 11 cm. – (Advancement of biological science series; 21)

Corporate Bodies Problem No. 50
Institution

MANUAL
of
MICROBIOLOGY

Prepared by
Committee on Bacteriological Technic
Society of American Bacteriologists

McGRAW – HILL BOOK COMPANY, Inc.
New York

1957

- Class No. G91
- Book No. J 7
- Page : i-ix and 1-365
- Size : 25½ x 11 ½ centimeters
- Advancement of Biological Science Series No. XXVIII
- Accession No. 122231
- Contains graphs, charts, diagrams, tables, etc.

G91
J 7

Society of American Bacteriologists. *Committee on Bacteriological Technic.*

Manual of microbiology / prepared by Committee on Bacteriological Technic, Society of American Bacteriologists. – New York : McGraw-Hill, 1957

ix, 365 p. : ill. ; 26 x 12 cm. (Advancement of biological science series; 28)

1. Microbiology – Handbooks, manuals, etc. 2. Title 3. series.

G91
J 7

MICROBIOLOGY – HANDBOOKS, MANUALS ...

Society of American Bacteriologists. *Committee on Bacteriological Technic.*

Manual of microbiology / prepared by Committee on Bacteriological Technic, Society of American Bacteriologists. – New York : McGraw-Hill, 1957

ix, 365 p. : ill. ; 26 x 12 cm. (Advancement of biological science series; 28)

G91 Manual of microbiology

J 7 Society of American Bacteriologists. *Committee on Bacteriological Technic.*

Manual of microbiology / prepared by Committee on Bacteriological Technic, Society of American Bacteriologist. – New York : McGraw-Hill, 1957.

ix, 365 p. : ill. ; 26 x 12 cm. (Advancement of biological science series; 28)

G91 Advancement of biological science series; 28.

J 7 Society of American Bacteriologists. *Committee on Bacteriological Technic.*

Manual of microbiology / prepared by Committee on Bacteriological Technic, Society of American Bacteriologist. – New York : McGraw-Hill, 1957.

ix, 365 p. : ill. ; 26 x 12 cm. (Advancement of biological science series; 28)

Corporate Bodies
Institute IIPA

Problem No. 51

THE INDIAN INSTITUTE OF PUBLIC ADMINISTRATION

New Delhi

The Organization of the Government of India

An Introductory Manual

Asia Publishing House
* Bombay * Calcutta * New Delhi
* London * New York

- Class No. W6,2.44
- Copy rights : June 1958
- Book No. J 8
- Thoroughly illustrated
- Contains a Select Bibliography from Pages 341 to 348. Class No. W6, 2. 44a
- Size : 23¼ x 13 ¼ centimeters
- Page : i-ix and 1-352
- Accession No. 112213

W6'2.44		
J 8	The Indian Institute of Public Administration, *New Delhi.*	
	The organization of the government of India : an introductory manual. – Bombay; London; New York : Asia Publishing House, °1958.	
112213	ix, 352 p. : ill. ; 24 cm.	
	Select bibliography : p. 341-348.	
	1. India – government organization 2. Title	

W6'2.44		INDIA – GOVERNMENT ORGANISATION
J 8	The Indian Institute of Public Administration, *New Delhi.*	
	The organization of the government of India : an introductory manual. – Bombay; London; New York : Asia Publishing House, °1958.	
	ix, 352 p. : ill. ; 24 cm.	
	Select bibliography : p. 341-348.	

W6'2.44		The Organisation of the government of India.
J 8	The Indian Institute of Public Administration, *New Delhi.*	
	The organization of the government of India : an introductory manual. – Bombay; London; New York : Asia Publishing House, °1958.	
	ix, 352 p. : ill. ; 24 cm.	
	Select bibliography : p. 341-348.	

Corporate Bodies Problem No. 52
Institution : League of Nations

Economic, Financial and Transit Department

TRADE RELATIONS BETWEEN FREE MARKETS AND CONTROLLED ECONOMICS

LEAGUE OF NATIONS
Geneva

1943

- Class No. X5:8
- Book No. H3
- Page : i-ix and 1-350
- Accession No. 124531
- Size : 27½ x 11 ½ centimeters

X5:8	
H 3	League of Nations. *Economic Financial and Transit Department, Geneva.*
	Trade relations between free markets and controlled economics / League of Nations, economic financial and transit department. – Geneva : League of Nations, 1943.
124531	ix, 350 p. ; 28 x 12 cm.
	1. Free-Market trade 2. Controlled economics 3. Title

X5:8	FREE—MARKET TRADE
H 3	League of Nations. *Economic Financial and Transit Department, Geneva.*
	Trade relations between free markets and controlled economics / League of Nations, economic financial and transit department. – Geneva : League of Nations, 1943.
	ix, 350 p. ; 28 x 12 cm.

X5:8		CONTROLLED ECONOMICS
H 3	League of Nations. *Economic Financial and Transit Department, Geneva.*	
	Trade relations between free market and controlled economics / League of Nations, economic financial and transit department. – Geneva : League of Nations, 1943.	
	ix, 350 p. ; 28 x 12 cm.	
	○	

X5:8		Trade relations between free markets and ...
H 3	League of Nations. *Economic Financial and Transit Department, Geneva.*	
	Trade relations between free markets and controlled economics / League of Nations, economic financial and transit department. – Geneva : League of Nations, 1943.	
	ix, 350 p. ; 28 x 12 cm.	
	○	

Serials & Periodicals Problem No. 53

BRITISH PSYCHOLOGIST

Vol. I — No. 1

January – March,
1916

Sponsored by
British Society of Psychologists
LONDON

- Class No. Sm56, N16
- 4 issues in a calendar year form one volume
- Library started subscription from Vol. No. 4
- No volume published in 1919
- Library lacks volume No. 15
- In 1941 the title of the periodical changed to 'Modern Psycho-Physicist' Class No. S:5m56, N41.
- No change in Sponsoring Body and 4 issues to form one complete volume.
- Vol. 9 is not available in the library.
- Size : 22 centimeters
- Due to financial problem, publication of periodical stopped.

ROUGH WORK

Year	Vol.	
1916	01	
1917	02	
1918	03	
1919	04	Library started subscription
1920	05	No. Vol. published
1921	06	
1922	07	
1923	08	
1924	09	
1925	10	
1926	11	
1927	12	
1928	13	
1929	14	
1930	15	Vol. not available
1931	16	
1932	17	
1933	18	
1934	19	
1935	20	
1936	21	
1937	22	
1938	23	
1939	24	
1940	01	Modern Psycho-physicist (Title changed.
1941	02	New Vol. numbering started)
1942	03	
1943	04	
1944	05	
1945	06	
1946	07	
1947	08	
1948	09	Vol. not available
1949	10	
1950	11	
1951	12	Periodical stopped

Sm56,N16	British Psychologist / British Society of Psychologists. – Vol. 4 (1919). – London : British Society of Psychologists, 1916-1939.
	20 V. ; 22 cm.
	Quarterly.
	No. Vol. published in 1920.
	Vol. 15 (1930) not available
	Continued by : Modern psycho-physicist.
	1. Psychology – periodicals. 2. British Society of Psychologists.

Sm56,N16	PSYCHOLOGY – PERIODICALS
	British Psychologist / British Society of Psychologists. – Vol. 4 (1919). – London : British Society of Psychologists, 1916-1939.
	20 V.; 22 cm.
	Quarterly.
	No. Vol. published in 1920.
	Vol. 15 (1930) not available
	Continued by : Modern psycho-physicist.

Sm56,N16	British Society of Psychologists
	British Psychologist / British Society of Psychologists. – Vol. 4 (1919). – London : British Society of Psychologists, 1916-1939.
	20 V. ; 22 cm.
	Quarterly.
	No. Vol. published in 1920.
	Vol. 15 (1930) not available
	Continued by : Modern psycho-physicist.

Sm56,N41

Modern psycho-physicist / British Society of Psychologists. – Vol. 1. (1940). – Vol. 12 (1951).

12 V. ; 22 cm.

Quarterly.

Vol. 9 (1948) not available.

1. Psychophysics – periodicals. 2. British Society of Psychologists.

S: 5m56, N41 PSYCHOPHYSICS – PERIODICALS

Modern psycho-physicist / British Society of Psychologists. – Vol. 1. (1940). – Vol. 12 (1951).

12 V. ; 22 cm.

Quarterly.

Vol. 9 (1948) not available.

S: 5m56, N41 British Society of Psychologists.

Modern psycho-physicist / British Society of Psychologists. – Vol. 1. (1940). – Vol. 12 (1951).

12 V. ; 22 cm.

Quarterly.

Vol. 9 (1948) not available.

Serials & Periodicals
With Complexities

Problem No. 54

QUARTERLY JOURNAL OF WORLD HISTORY

Vol. I :: No. 1 Jan – Mar 1953

Sponsored by
American Historical Society
CHICAGO

- Class No. Vm73,N53
- Library is subscribing the Journal from the first volume.
- 4 issues in a calendar year form one volume
- No volumes were published in 1956 and 1957
- In 1970, the title of the Journal was changed to Journal of World Culture", Class No. Y:1m73,N73, with no change in periodicity and Sponsoring body. New Vol. numbering started.
- In 1978, from Jan-Mar. issue, the Journal was split into :

  (a) Cultural Trends (Class No. Y:1m73,N78,1)

  (b) Civilization Trends (Class No. Y:1m73,N78,2)
- The Sponsoring Body and periodicity remained unchanged. New Vol. numbering started.
- The Library does not possess Vol. 14 of Cultural Trends.
- No Vol. of Civilization Trends published in 2001.
- Size : 22 centimeters.
- Library stopped subscription after 2005.

Vm73,N53	Quarterly journal of world history / American	
		Historical Society. – Vol. 1 (1953). – Chicago : American Historical Society, 1953-1970.
		16 V. ; 22 cm.
		No. Vol. published in 1956 and 1957.
		Continued by : Journal of world culture.
		1. World history – Periodicals. 2. American
	Historical Society.	

Vm73,N53		WORLD HISTORY – PERIODICALS
	Quarterly journal of world history / American	
		Historical Society. – Vol. 1 (1953). – Chicago : American Historical Society, 1953-1970.
		16 V. ; 22 cm.
		No. Vol. published in 1956 and 1957.
		Continued by : Journal of world culture.

Vm73,N53		American Historical Society
	Quarterly journal of world history / American	
		Historical Society. – Vol. 1 (1953). – Chicago : American Historical Society, 1953-1970.
		16 V. ; 22 cm.
		No. Vol. published in 1956 and 1957.
		Continued by : Journal of world culture.

Y:1m73,N70 Journal of world culture / American Historical Society. Vol. 1 (1970). – V. 8 (1977).– Chicago : American Historical Society, 1970-1977.

8 V. ; 22 cm.

Quarterly.

Split into : Cultural trends, and : Civilization trends.

Library lacks Vol. 14 (1991)

1. Culture – periodicals. 2. American Historical Society. ○

Y:1m73,N70 CULTURE – PERIODICALS

Journal of world culture / American Historical Society. Vol. 1 (1970). – V. 8 (1977).– Chicago : American Historical Society, 1970-1977.

8 V. ; 22 cm.

Quarterly.

Split into : Cultural trends, and : Civilization trends.

Library lacks Vol. 14 (1991)

Y:1m7 3,N70 American Historical Society.

Journal of world culture / American Historical Society. – Vol. 1 (1970). —Vol. 8 (1977). – Chicago : American Historical Society, 1970-1977.

8 V. ; 22 cm.

Quarterly.

Y:1m73, N78,1

Cultural trends / American Historical Society. – Vol. 1 (1978) – Vol.26 (2005). – Chicago : American Historical Society, 1978-2005.

26 V. ; 22 cm.

Quarterly.

Library lacks Vol. 14 (1991)

1. Culture – periodicals. 2. American Historical Society

Y:1m73,N78,1 CULTURE – PERIODICALS

Cultural trends / American Historical Society. – Vol. 1 (1978) – Vol. 26 (2005). – Chicago : American Historical Society, 1978-2005.

26 V. ; 22 cm.

Quarterly.

Library lacks Vol. 14 (1991)

Y:1m73,N78,1 American Historical Society

Cultural trends / American Historical Society. Vol. 1 (1978) – Vol. 26 (2005). – Chicago : American Historical Society, 1978-2005.

26 V. ; 22 cm.

Quarterly.

Library lacks Vol. 14 (1991)

Y:1m73, N78,2		Civilization trends / American Historical Society. – Vol. 1 (1978) – Vol. 26 (2005). – Chicago : American Historical Society, 1978-2005. 26 V.. ; 22 cm. Quarterly. No Vol. published in 2001. 1. Civilization – periodicals. 2. American Historical Society.

Y:1m73, N782,2		CIVILIZATION – PERIODICALS Civilization trends / American Historical Society. Vol. 1 (1978). – Vol. 26 (2005). – Chicago : American Historical Society, 1978-2005. 26 V. ; 22 cm. Quarterly. No Vol. published in 2001.

Y:1m73, N782,2		American Historical Society Civilization trends / American Historical Society. Vol. 1 (1978). – Vol. 26 (2006). – Chicago : American Historical Society, 1978–2005. 26 V. ; 22 cm. Quarterly. No Vol. published in 2001.

Appendix
Rendering of Names of Prominent Authors

Aatish, Khwaja Haider Ali, 1846
Abdul Ghaffar, Qazi, 1888-1956
Abdul Haq, Maulana, 1870-1961
Abdul Qadir, Sheikh, 1878-1950
Abid Husain, Syed, 1899
Afsar Ali Mairathi, Hamidullah, 1898
Agha Hashar Kaashmiri, 1879-1936
Ahsan Mareharvi, Syed Ali Ahsan, 1875-1940
Akbar Allahabadi, Syed Akbar Husain, 1846-1921
Akbar, Jalaluddin Mohammad, Mughal Emperor, 1556-1605
Aman, Gopi Nath
Ameer Meinai, Ameer Ahmad, 1832-1900
Anis, Meer Babbar Ali, 1802-1874
Asghar Gondvi, Asghar Husain, 1884-1936
Ashraf Jehangir Samnani, Syed Mohd., 1289-1405
Ayyub Khan, President of Pakistan, 1960-1966
Azad, Maulvi Mohd. Husain, 1832-1910
Azad, Mohiuddin Ahmad Maulana Abul Kalam, 1888-1958

Babur, Zahiruddin Muhammad, Mughal Emperor, 1494-15...
Bandanawaz Gesoo Draz, Syed Mohd. Al-Huseni Khawaja, 1320-1412
Burhanuddin Janam, Shah, 1582
Chakbast, Brij Narain, 1882-1926
Chiragh Ali, Maulvi, 1846-1895
Daagh, Nawab Mirza Khan, 1831-1905
Dard, Khwaja Meer, 1719-1785
Fani Badauni, 1880-1941
Farhat Ullah Beg, Mirza, 1886-1946
Gandhi, Mohandas Karam Chand, 1869-1948
Ghalib, Mirza Asadullah Khan, 1797-1869
Ghulamul Saqlain, Khawaja,
Hafeez Jalandhari, 1900
Hali, Khwaja Altaf Husain, 1837-1914
Hasan Nizami, Khawaja, 1878-1955
Hasrat Mohani, Syed Faziul Hasan, 1875-1951
Hatim, Shah Zahooruddin, 1699-1791
Ibrahim Adil Shah Sani, Sultan Bijapur, 1580-1626
Iqbal, Sir Sheikh Mohd. Iqbal, 1873-1938
Ismail Dehalvi, Maulvi, 1796-1831
Ismail Mairathi, Maulvi Mohd. Ismail, 1844-1917
Jalal Lakhnawi, Hakim Syed Zamin Ali, 1834-1909
Jauhar, Mohd. Ali, 1878-1931
Jigar Moradabadi, Ali Sikandar, 1890-1960
Josh Malihabadi, Shabbir Hasan Khan, 1894
Josh, Sultan Haider, 1954
Kabir Das, 1440-1518
Kaifi, Pandit Brij Mohan Datatariya, 1866-1955
Kaul, Kishan Prasad, 1885-1955
Khusro, Abul Hasan Ameer, 1255-1325
Kirishan Chandra, 1914-1977

Meer, Taqi Meer, 1724-1810
Mohd. Quli Qutab Shah, Sultan Golkunda, 1580-1611
Mohsinul Mulk, Mehdi Ali Khan, 1837-1907
Momin, Mohd. Momin, Khan, 1800-1851
Nazeer Ahmad, Maulvi, 1836-1912
Nazeer Akbarabadi, Sheikh Wali Mohd. 1740-1830
Nehru, Jawahar Lal, 1889-1964
Niaz Fatehpuri, Niaz Mohd. Khan, 1887
Nigam, Daya Narain, 1884-1903
Nizami, Khaleeq Ahmad
Prem Chand (Dhanpat Rai Srivastava), 1881-1936
Pustar, Ahmad Shah Bukhari, 1898
Raashidul Khair, Maulana, 1868-1936
Radhakrishnan, S., President of India, 1962-1967
Rajendra Prasad, President of India, 1950-1962
Ruswa, Mirza Mohd. Hadi, 1858-1936
Sarshar, Pandit Ratan Nath, 1847-1902
Sauda, Mirza Mohd. Rafi, 1713-1781
Shibli, Mohd. Shibli Naumani, 1875-1914
Siddiqui, Rasheed Ahmad, 1895
Siraj, Meer Sirajuddin, 1715-1761
Soz, Syed Mohd. Meer, 1720-1798
Sulaiman Nadvi, Syed 1884-1953
Syed Ahmad Khan, Sir, 1817-1898
Tagore, Rabindra Nath, 1861-1948
Zafar, Sirajuddin Mohd. Bahadur Shah 1775-1862
Zakaullah, Maulvi, 1832-1910
Zauq, Sheikh Mohd. Ibrahim, 1789-1854
Ziauddin Ahmad, Sir, 1877-1947

*** It may be noted that the years given for the President of Republic, Emperor, King, etc. are the years of tenure of the position held by them.

